" GAELIC MADE EASY "

A Guide to Gaelic for Beginners

PART 3

COMPRISING 10 LESSONS IN GAELIC
including VOCABULARY

Written and Compiled by
John M. Paterson

GAIRM PUBLICATIONS

First Edition...........................1958
Second Edition........................1963
Third Edition 1971
Fourth Edition 1991
Fifth Edition...........................1997
This impression......................2003

GAELIC MADE EASY PART 3

ISBN: 0-57970-550-2 text only
          0-88432-443-5 text and cassettes
          1-57970-124-8 text and cds

This edition published by Audio Forum
One Orchard Park Road, Madison, CT 06443 U.S.A.
www.audioforum.com

Printed in the United States of America

SOUND TABLE

A as in CAT. Never as in MATE.

E as in THEY or MET. Never as in ME.

I as in MACHINE or FIT. Never as in FIRE.

O as in GO or GOT.

U as in PUT or BUT. Never as in FUEL.

AO like EH-OO said quickly or like EU of NEUVE in French. An approximate sound is 'oo'.

PH as F. Compare PHOTO in English.

BH and MH as V in VAT.

CH as in LOCH.

DH and GH as GH in UGH! back in throat.

SH and TH as H in HAT.

FH is silent except in three words FHEIN (hayn) FHUAIR (hoo-ir) and FHATHAST (ha-hast) where it has the sound of H.

IS as IS in MISSION i.e. ISH but IS meaning 'is' is sounded ISS as in HISS.

SI as SI in MISSION i.e. SHI.

IDH and IGH as EE.

DHI and GHI as YE.

ANN sounds both 'Ns' though often sounded as if A-OON.

L before A, O, U like LL in CALLING or THL.

MH and BH often sounded like W in middle of word, though, like V would also be correct.

I and E, when the second letters of a word, often sound like Y, as DIURA (dyura) i.e. almost as a 'j' sound ; but when an action-word is in the past time this does not take place. LION! (lyeeon) FILL! but LION (leeon) FILLED.

Note.—We use the 'j' sound in the imitated pronunciation.

C in or at the end of a word is often sounded as CHK thus MAC as if it were MACHK, the CH of MACHK being as in LOCH.

CHD is also sounded as CHK. Thus BOCHD as BOCHK.

RT is often sounded as RST.

D and T. Get tongue well against back of upper front teeth. T is almost TH.

B. and P. With lips well pressed together.

G well back in throat. GOT would be like UGOT.

The accent in Gaelic always falls on the first syllable of the word.

IMITATED PRONUNCIATION

Sound CH as in LoCH, ch as in church. O as in sO,
o as in got, ich as in which; j as in jilt; ing as in
sing; ay as in day; oo as in moon.

Only approximate pronunciation has been aimed at.
Anything more complex or detailed would only confuse
the learner.

LESSON 21

When we wish to show that we are speaking of more than one person or thing, we generally add AN (or EAN) to the end of the name-word. Thus LOCH, 1. loch: LOCHAN, lochs. SGOIL, 2. school: SGOILEAN, schools. TAIGH, 1. house: TAIGHEAN, houses. AN ORDAG, 2. The thumb: NA H-ORDAGAN, The thumbs, and so on. You will notice that when the last vowel of the name-word was "I" we added EAN to the end of the name-word; and further, how NA became NA H- before vowels. In the same way we would say NA H-AINMEAN (na Henum-an), The names: NA H-IASGAIREAN (na Heeasg-ar-an), The fishermen: NA H-EAGLAISEAN (na Heklish-an), The churches: NA H-UIBHEAN (na Hooey-an), The eggs.

Sometimes we find name-words in the above form being shortened, or even altered and added to before adding AN (or EAN). But these changes are very simple. For instance, UBHAL (ooal) 1. apple: UBHLAN (oo-lan) apples. DORUS, 1. door: DORSAN, doors. CARAID (kar-ij) 1. friend: CAIRDEAN (kar-jan) friends. BEINN (bayng) 2. ben or peak: BEANNTAN (byaoon-tan) or BEANNT-AICHEAN (byaoon-ti-CHyan) bens or peaks. This long form is becoming very common nowadays. Thus BATA, 1. boat: BATAICHEAN (ba-ti-Chyan) boats. So also LEABHRAICHEAN (lyO-ri-CHyan) books from LEABHAR (lyOr) 1. book. LOCH, 1. loch has LOCHAN and LOCHANNAN, lochs. Often the sound is softened by putting an "I" into the word which makes us add EAN and not AN. For example, BUTH (boo) 1. shop: BUTHAN (boo-an) or BUITHEAN

1

(**boo-yan**) shops. RATHAD, 1. road, has RATH-
AIDEAN (**ra-ee-jan**). LA, 1. day: LAITHEAN
(**la-yan**) days. NI (**nyee**) 1. thing: NITHEAN (**nyee-
an**). Note how -TH was put in to separate vowels, in
this case I and E. So also CNO (**cro**) 2. nut:
CNOTHAN (**cro-an**) nuts. POSADH (**pos-uGH**) 1.
marriage: POSAIDHEAN (**pos-ee-yan**) marriages.
Words which end in ADH go the same way as
POSADH.

There is another way of showing that we mean more
than one person or thing and that is by making a
change in the middle of the name-word. Now we find
this already in English. For example, MAN becomes
MEN, GOOSE becomes GEESE and MOUSE becomes
MICE. The change we have spoken of is due to an
"I" being put into the name-word in Gaelic. Thus
CAT, 1. cat becomes CAIT (**ka-eech**) cats. RAMH
(**rav**) 1. oar: RAIMH (**ra-eev**) oars. ORAN (**oran**)
1. song: ORAIN (**or-ayn**) songs. SASUNNACH, 1.
Englishman: SASUNNAICH (**sasun-eeCH**) English-
men. MAC (**maCHk**) I. son, has got shortened to
MIC (**meeCHk**) sons.

This putting in of the letter "I" has caused some
curious changes in words whose central sound is A, O,
EA, EO, EU, IA. Here are some of these: CARN, 1.
heap: CUIRN (**kooirn**) heaps, CLAG, 1. bell: CLUIG
(**klooig**) bells, BALG (**balug**) 1. bag or wallet: BUILG
(**booil-ug**) bags or wallets. Likewise BORD, 1. table:
BUIRD (**booird**) tables. TONN (**town**) 1. wave:
TUINN (**too-ing**) waves. PORT (**port**) 1. tune, harbour
or inlet: PUIRT (**pooirt**) tunes, harbours or inlets. In
some places IRT and IRD are sounded as "irst".

EA words are shortened to "I" or "EI". CEANN
(**kyaoon**) 1. head: CINN (**keeng**) heads. FEAR
(**fer**) 1. man: FIR (**feer**) men. CLEIREACH (**klay-
raCH**) 1. clerk: CLEIRICH (**klay-reeCH**) clerks. But
notice EACH (**eCH**) 1. horse: EICH (**ay-eech**) horses.

EU words change EU to EOI. Thus BEUL (**bayl**) 1.
mouth: BEOIL (**byo-il**) mouths. EUN (**ay-un**) 1. bird:
EOIN (**yo-in**) birds.

Lastly IA words change IA to EI. For example IASG

(eeask) 1. fish: EISG (ayshk) fishes. FIADH (fee-uGH) 1. a deer: FEIDH (fay-ee) deer.

There are two very common words that are worth careful notice. DUINE (doon-ya) 1. man: DAOINE (deh-oon-ya) men. Again BEAN (ben) 2. woman: but MNATHAN (mra-han) women.

Usually MN and CN are sounded as MR and CR at the beginning of a word. For example CNOC, a hill is sounded as "kroCHk" although we still find the "N" sounded in Uist.

In general it may be said that those words that change in the middle to show more than one person or thing (and they are not many) almost always belong to Class 1 or what the grammars call "masculine". The usual way of showing more than one person or thing is, as we have said above, by adding AN (or EAN) to the end of the name-word.

Faclair

THAIRIS AIR (harish er) over, across.
ADAG 2. stook or shock of corn; or haddock.
ADAGAN, stooks of corn; also haddocks.
ALLT (aoolt) 1. burn or mountain stream.
UILLT (oo-eelch) burns or mountain streams.
SGRIOSAIL (sgreesal) destructive.
GLAC! (glaCHk) catch!
NAOI (nooee) nine.
BREAC (breCHk) 1. a trout.
BRIC (breeCHk) trout or of a trout.
SLOAD! (slood) drag!
CAISG (kaashk) 2. Easter, usually written A' CHAISG
  (a CHaeeshk) (the) Easter.
COIN (kOin) 1. dogs.
CAISG! (keshk) check! restrain! staunch!
CAORA (koora) 2. a sheep.
CAORAICH (koo-reeCH) 2. sheep.
GLEANN (glya-oon) 1. glen.
GLINN (gleeng) 1. glens; also GLEANNTAN
  (glyaoon-tan).
LOISG! (lOshk) burn!
MARBH! (mar uv) kill!
MANACH (man-aCH) 1. monk.

MANAICH (**man-eeCH**) monks.
BAS (**bass**) 2. palm of hand.
BASAN, palms.
BUAIL! (**boo-ayl**) strike! clap!
NEAD (**nyed**) 1. nest.
NID (**nyeej**) nests.
REIC (**rayCHk**) 2. sale.
BLAIDHNAIL (**bleea-nal**) yearly.
BUITHEAN-AODAICH (**boo-yan ood-eeCH**)
    1. Draper-shops.
GEARR-OSAIN (**gyar-ossayn**) 1. socks.
LEINE (**lyay-na**) 2. shirt.
LEINTEAN (**lyayn-chan**) shirts.
TRUSGAN-CADAIL (**troosgan kad-il**) 1. pyjamas.
GU MATH, well, fairly.
SAOR (**soor**) cheap.
CROM! (**krOm**) bend! also crooked.
FHAD'S A (**ads-a**) whilst.
TROD (**trod**) scolding.
TROID! (**troj**) scold! followed by RI, at.

Gaelic to English

Bha an sneachd trom air na cnuic. Chaidh na h-eich
thairis air an abhainn. Dh'fhalbh na h-adagan leis na
h-uilt. Co as a tha na daoine sin? Tha iad as (or a)
Muile: is Muilich iad. Sheinn na cluig an uair a thill
na saighdearan o'n chogadh. Tha na cogaidhean sgriosail. Ghlac na balaich naoi bric anns an t-sruth. Shlaod
na fir na bataichean gu taobh an uisge. Chaisg an
tuathanach na coin: bha iad ris na caoraich. Nach
boidheach na beanntan agus na glinn agus na lochan
anns an duthaich seo! Loisg na Lochlannaich na
leabhraichean a fhuair iad anns na h-eaglaisean agus
mharbh iad na manaich. Tha mi a' faicinn gum bheil
na saoir trang ris na taighean ud agus tha e coltach
gum bi iad deas aig a' Chaisg. An uair a bhuail na
gillean am basan dh' eirich na h-eoin as an nid. Is e
an reic bhliadhnail a bh'ann anns na buithean-aodaich
an Glaschu an la roimhe. An do cheannaich do bhrathair dad? Cheannaich e gearr-osain, cota mor, leintean
agus trusgan-cadail. Fhuair e gu math saor iad. Chrom

4

na sgoilearan an cinn fhad's a bha am maighstir a' trod riutha.

Translation

The snow was heavy on the hills. The horses went over the river. The stooks of corn went off down (with) the burns. From where are those men? They are from Mull: they are Mullmen. The bells rang when the soldiers returned from the war. Wars are destructive. The boys caught nine trout in the stream. The men dragged the boats to the side of the water. The farmer checked the dogs: they were at the sheep. Aren't the bens and glens and lochs beautiful in this country! The Vikings burned the books that they found in the churches and they killed the monks. I see that the joiners are busy at those houses and it is likely that they will be ready at Easter. When the boys clapped their hands the birds rose out their nests. It's the yearly sale that was on in the draper-shops in Glasgow the other day. Did your brother buy anything? He bought socks, a great-coat, shirts and pyjamas. He got them fairly cheap. The scholars bent their heads while the master was scolding them.

LESSON 22

The study of Place-names is very interesting. Not only do they describe the appearance of a place but often they recall some historical event. Mostly however they are descriptive and very practical. Take for instance the word INISHFREE, which means Island of Heather, and, by the way, is the title of a well-known poem. The name is made up from INNIS (**inyish**) 2. island and FRAOCH (**frooCH**) 1. heather. To show "of heather" in Gaelic we put an "i" into FRAOCH which now becomes FRAOICH (**froo-eeCH**). Thus the name would be written INNIS FRAOICH.

BALLACHULISH. This well-known Highland town is famed for the excellence of its slates which last for centuries. The word is made up from BAILE (**bala**) 1. town and CAOLAS (**koo-las**) 1. strait or narrows. Written in full in Gaelic it would be BAILE AN CHAOLAIS, The Town of the Narrows or more shortly now BAILE A' CHAOLAIS. Notice that of the two "the's" the first one, in this case before BAILE, is not translated in Gaelic. This is a rule. Thus CEANN AN RATHAID, (The) head (or end) of the road. Then again, the first letter of CAOLAIS was sharpened by putting an "H" after it. This sharpening takes place with "of" forms wherever possible after AN (or AM), that is, with words belonging to Class 1, the masculines of the grammars. Where however we do not put in an "H" as in RATHAID above, we must write AN and not A'. So we have BAILE A' CHAOLAIS (**bal' a Choolaysh**).

TAYVALLICH. This comes from TAIGH (**ta-ee**) house and BEALACH (**byal-aCH**) 1. a pass. In Gaelic it is written TAIGH A' BHEALAICH (**ta-ee a vyal-**

6

eeCH), The House of the Pass. AM like AN becomes A', as we said before.

DRUMANTAGGART. This is in Gaelic DRUIM AN T-SAGAIRT, and means The Ridge of the Priest. It comes from DRUIM (**drooeem**) 1. ridge or back, and SAGART (**sagart**) 1. priest. You will notice that we wrote AN T-SAGAIRT and not AN SHAGAIRT or A' SHAGAIRT. Words belonging to Class 1 and beginning with S followed by a vowel or L, N, R, do not sharpen the S but instead put in a "T" which destroys the sound of the S. The place-name is therefore DRUIM AN T-SAGAIRT (**drooeem an tag-ayrt**), The ridge of the priest.

Here is an interesting name, COLINTRAIVE. This beautiful spot on the Kyles of Bute is named from two words CAOL (**kool**) 1. which like CAOLAS means a narrow passage, and SNAMH (**snav**) 1. swimming. The Gaelic form of the word is CAOL AN T-SNAIMH (**kool an trayv**), The Strait of the Swimming. It got this name because in former times the drovers used to swim their cattle across at this point. The word KYLES by the way is just CAOLAS and KYLE is CAOL. Note also how the difficult sound (T(S)N) has been pronounced as "tr".

Let us now consider Place-names whose second part is a word belonging to Class 2. TIGHNABRUAICH, a well-known holiday resort on the Kyles of Bute, is a good example. In Gaelic this is TAIGH NA BRUAICHE meaning The House of (i.e. standing on) the Bank which exactly describes the town which has grown up around it. TAIGH, house and BRUACH (**brooaCH**) 2. bank. As BRUACH belongs to Class 2 we use NA instead of A' for the "of" form of "The", and besides putting in an "I" we add an "E" at the end and so we get NA BRUAICHE. The correct pronunciation of TAIGH NA BRUAICHE (**ta-ee na brooeeCHa**) has been a bit ill-treated in the English.

The Inverness-shire town of DRUMNADROCHIT gets its name from DRUIM, ridge and DROCHAID (**droCH-ij**) 2. a bridge. Correctly written it is DRUIM

7

NA DROCHAIDE (**drooeem na droCHij-a**), The Ridge of (or by) the Bridge. Here we needed only to add an "E" as there was an "I" already in DRÒCHAID.

In our last lesson we saw how the putting of an "I" into a word might make changes in the sound. For instance CARN, 1. heap or cairn became CUIRN, heaps or cairns. BORD, table, became BUIRD, tables. FEAR, man, became FIR, men, but EACH, horse, became EICH, horses. BEUL, mouth, became BEOIL, mouths, and IASG, fish, became EISG, fishes. Now, as we also put in an "I" to get the "of" form of the name-word we might expect to find the same changes ; and this is just what happens. Here are a few examples:

CARN, 1. cairn. CUIRN, of a cairn. FEAR-CUIRN, an outlaw, i.e. man of a cairn.

AIR MULLACH A' CHUIRN (**CHooirn**), On (the) top of the cairn.

BORD, 1. Board, table. CEANN A' BHUIRD (**vooird**), The head of the table.

CEARC, 2. hen. UBH CIRCE (**kirCH-ka**), a hen's egg. ITEAN NA CIRCE, The feathers of the hen.

EACH, 1. horse. MUING EICH, a horse's mane. EARBALL AN EICH, The tail of the horse.

FEAR, 1. man. AINM FIR, A man's name. AINM AN FHIR (**enum an yeer**), The name of the man.

BEUL, 1. mouth. DORUS BEOIL, Front door, i.e. Door of mouth. TAOBH MO BHEOIL (**vyo-il**), The side of my mouth.

IASG, 1. fish. LANNAN AGUS ITEAN AN EISG, The scales and the fins of the fish. (Pron. AN EISG as 'an yayshk').

CEOL, 1. music. FEAR CIUIL, musician, i.e. man of music. LUATHAS A' CHIUIL, The speed of the music. CHIUIL (**CHyooil**).

MULLACH (**mool-aCH**) 1. top, summit. ITE (**eecha**) 2. feather, quill, fin. MUING (**mooing**) 2. mane of horse. EARBALL (**erub-al**) 1. tail. LANN (**la-oon**) 2. scale, blade. LUATHAS (**looas**) 1. speed.

Note how we said AN FHIR (**an yeer**) not A' FHIR (**an eer**) the N being kept in between the two vowels. In the same way we say in English An idea not A idea.

There are a few odd words we may mention. MACHAIR (maCH-ir) 2. a wet meadow becomes MACHRACH (maCH-raCH) of a wet meadow. So also OBAIR, 2. work. OBRACH of work. MATHAIR (ma-hir) 2. mother. MATHAR, 2 (ma-har) of a mother. ATHAIR (a-hir) 1. father and BRATHAIR (bra-hir) 1. brother also drop their "I". PIUTHAR (pyoo-har) 2. sister. PEATHAR (peh-har) of a sister. LOCH, 1. loch gives LOCHA. FUIL (fooil) 2. blood. FALA, of blood. DUTHAICH (doo-eeCH) 2. country. DUTHCHA (doo-CHa) of a country. MADUINN (ma-ting) 2. MAIDNE (maj-na) of a morning. MAC (maCHk) 1. son. MIC (meeCHk) of a son.

Faclair

BONN (bown) 1. sole; also coin, medal.
FAD, during; followed by "of" forms.
UINE (ooinya) 2. time, period.
CUL (cool) 1. back.
CORP, 1. body.
BUN (boon) 1. bottom, base.
GLAC! (glaCHk) catch!
ANN AN (or AM) in.
POLL (powl) 1. pool.
DOMHAIN (do-in) deep.
CEANN (kyaoon) 1. head, end.
ACHADH (aCH-uGH) 1. field.
LEAC (lyeCHk) 2. flat stone, flagstone.
GRIAN (greean) 2. sun.
TEAS (chess) 1. heat.
SGAIL (ska-il) 2. shade, shadow.
BUNAIT (boon-ich) 2. foundation.
NEART (nyarst) 1. force, strength.
LEUM! (lyaym) leap!
LEUM (laym) leapt.
LEUM 1. a leap.
LEIM, of a leap.
MUIN (moon short) 1. back.
FAOBHAR (foovar) 1. edge.
SGIAN, 2. knife.
GEUR (gayr) sharp.
GEARR! (gyarr) cut!

CORRAG (**kor-rag**) 2. finger.
ABHAINN 2. river has AIBHNE (**evn-ya**) for its "of"
form.
RE (**ray**) for, during.

Gaelic to English

Stad an car re tri uairean aig Taigh an Uillt. Is mise
Iain Mac an t-Saoir. Tha bonn mo bhroige briste.
Bhruidhinn e fad na h-uine gun stad. Ruith i eadar an
dorus beoil agus an dorus cuil. Fhuair iad corp a'
bhalaich aig bun na creige. Togaibh i, togaibh i, canain
ar duthcha: is i sin a' Ghaidhlig. Ghlac na h-iasgairean
pailteas eisg ann am poll domhain aig ceann an locha.
Rinn iad rathad eadar Baile an t-sagairt agus Achadh
na lice. Bha teas na greine ro mhor agus shuidh iad
fo sgail na craoibhe. Cheannaich mac mo pheathar
leabhar-ciuil anns a' bhuth aig ceann na sraide. Cha
robh bunait na drochaide ro laidir agus thuit an drochaid le neart an t-srutha agus na gaoithe. Bha nighean
mo bhrathar a' cluich ri taobh na h-aibhne. Leum e air
muin an eich. Bha faobhar na sgeine geur agus ghearr
i barr a corraige.

Translation

The car stopped for three hours at Taynuilt. I am
John Macintyre. The sole of my shoe is broken. He
spoke throughout the period (all the time) without stop.
She ran between the front door and the back door.
They found the boy's body at the foot of the rock. Up
with it (lift it up), up with it, the language of our
country: that is the Gaelic. The fishermen caught
plenty of fish in a deep pool at the head of the loch.
They made a road between Balantaggart and Auchin-
leck. The heat of the sun was very great and they sat
under the shade of the tree. My sister's son (nephew)
bought a music book in the shop at the end of the
street. The foundation of the bridge wasn't very strong
and the bridge fell with the force of the current and
the wind. My brother's daughter (niece) was playing
at the side of the river. He leapt on the back of the
horse. The edge of the knife was sharp and she cut
the top of her finger.

10

LESSON 23

We have already seen how to turn into Gaelic a name-word when it is preceded by "of" and when it refers to ONE person or thing. Thus CLUICH BALAICH, A boy's game i.e. Game of a boy: CLUICHEAN BALAICH, A boy's games or games of a boy. Again CLUICH A' BHALAICH, The boy's game or (The) game of the boy.

If more than one boy is spoken about we turn our phrase into Gaelic as follows:

1. CLUICHEAN BHALACH, Boys' games or Games of boys.
2. CLUICHEAN NAM BALACH, The boys' games or (The) games of the boys.

What we did in (1) was to take the word for one boy and sharpen the first letter, B, to get the word for "of boys". In (2) we put NAM in front of BALACH without sharpening the B. Here are some other examples:

Take BROG, 2. shoes and FEAR, 1. man.

BROGAN FHEAR, Men's shoes. BROGAN NAM FEAR, The men's shoes or (The) shoes of the men. Note that FHEAR sounds "err", FH being silent.

NAN (or NAM before B, F, M, P) meaning "of the" is used before a name-word referring to more than one person or thing. Do not mix it up with NAN (NAM) meaning "if", which is used before an action-word.

Take BARR, 1. top. CRAOBH (kroov) 2. tree.

BARRAN CHRAOBH (Chroov), Tops of trees. BARRAN NAN CRAOBH, (The) tops of the trees.

So also with MUING (mooing) 2. mane of a horse and EACH (eCH) 1. horse. MUINGEAN EACH,

11

Horses' manes. MUINGEAN NAN EACH, (The) manes of the horses. Note that we cannot sharpen a vowel, so we just leave MUINGEAN EACH as it is.

There is a difference, however, for name-words of MORE than one syllable, excepting those ending in "ACH".

Take for example CAISBHEART (**kash-art**) 1. footwear i.e. boots and stockings, and CAILEAG, 2. a girl. CAISBHEART CHAILEAGAN, Girls' footwear: CAISBHEART NAN CAILEAGAN, The Girls' footwear or (The) footwear of the girls. Now if we had used CHAILEAG and NAN CAILEAG we would not have been wrong but this is unusual. Here are some further examples of the "of" forms. You will see that the Gaelic usage is a little different from that of English.

BHA AN GILLE A' GLANADH NAM BROG. The boy was cleaning the shoes, i.e. The boy was cleaning (of) the shoes.

THA MAIRI A' CUR AN ARAIN AIR A' BHORD. Mary is putting (of) the bread on the table.

CHAIDH AN CLEIREACH A THOGAIL A' MHAIL. The clerk went to lift the rent, i.e. The clerk went to lifting of the rent.

Remember A' TOGAIL, lifting: A THOGAIL, to lift or to lifting. The first A' was AIG, at, and the second A was from DO, to, and this sharpens the first letter of the next word if possible.

Descriptive Words

When a name-word refers to more than one person or thing, the describing word has an "A" tacked on to its end or an "E" if the last letter of the describing word is an "I".

Thus: GILLE MOR, a big boy: GILLEAN MORA, big boys. GILLE GLIC, a wise boy: GILLEAN GLICE, wise boys. GLIC (**gleeCHk**) wise. CAILEAG BHEAG, a little girl: CAILEAGAN BEAGA, little girls.

Notice that the describing word, which in this case is BEAGA, is not sharpened. So also, CAILEAG

GHLIC, a wise girl: CAILEAGAN GLICE, wise girls.

If, however, the describing word has more than one syllable or if it ends in a vowel, then make no change, e.g. CAILEAGAN BOIDHEACH, bonny girls. RATH-AIDEAN FADA, long roads. UAIREAN SONA, happy hours. UAIR (**ooir**) 2. hour. SONA (**sona**) happy. But notice carefully the following examples:

FIR MHORA, big men. BUIRD FHADA, long tables. When the name-word has an "I" as last vowel in the form for more than one person or thing, then the describing word has its first letter sharpened if possible. Thus MHORA and FHADA.

In a phrase where more than one "of" form occurs, only the last one is put into Gaelic.

BHA E A' TOGAIL CAS (not COISE) A' BHUIRD, he was lifting the leg of the table.

AIR MULLACH CNOC UAMH NAM FEAR, On the Top of The Hill of the Cave of the Men. UAMH (**oo-av**) 2. cave: UAMHA (**ooav-a**) of a cave. In this Islay place-name neither CNOC nor UAMH was put in the "of" form.

Faclair

GAIDHLIG (**ga-lig**) 2. Gaelic.
BEURLA (**bayr-la**). BEURLA SHASUNNACH (**bayr-la hass-oo-naCH**) 2. English language.
SHASUNNACH is often left out.
EADAR-THEANGACHADH (**edar-heng-aCH-uGH**) 1. translation. Stress "**heng**".
AM MEASG (**maysk**) in midst of, among: takes "of" forms.
SALM (**sal-um**) 2. psalm.
GUTH (**goo**) 1. voice, vote, mention.
AN AIRD AN EAR (**un arj un yerr**) The East.
EISDEACHD (**aysh-dyaCHk**) listening.
FUAIM (**foo-aym**) 1. or 2. sound.
CHI (**CHee**) see or shall see.
SNAIGEAR (**snayk-er**) 1. prowler, rascal.
TAIGH EIRIDINN (**ayr-ij-ing**) hospital 2.
AIR BHO'N DE (**er von jay**) day before yesterday.

13

SEALGAIR (**shalug-er**) 1. hunter.
LORG (**lor-ug**) 2. track, trace.
ALLT (**aoolt**) 1. burn.
UILLT (**ooilch**) of a burn.
TOGAIL OIRNN (**tOk-il or-ing**) lifting on us, i.e. going off.
IS FHEARR (**sherr**) 'tis better.
CATHAIR (**ka-hir**) 2. chair.
CATHRACH (**ka-raCH**) of a chair.
CATHRAICHEAN (**kar-eeCH-an**) chairs.
IOSAL (**ees-ul**) low.

Gaidhlig Gu Beurla

Cota fir. Cota an fhir. Cotaichean fhear. Cotaichean nam fear. Creag ard. Creagan arda. Mullach na creige. Mullach nan creag. Each glas. Eich ghlasa. Sgeulachd nan each glasa. Taigh a' bhodaich. Taighean nam bodach. Am measg nam bodach. Oran binn. Oran bhinne. Leabhar oran binne. Cas cathrach. Cas na cathrach. Casan nan cathraichean iosal. Salm. Leabhar nan salm. Ceud Leabhar nan Righ. Long mhor nan seol donna. Poll nam bradan. Ceann poll nam bradan. Guth fear na cathrach.

Co bha a' tilgeadh chlach. Bha na gillean beaga ud. Thainig na Fir Ghlice o'n Aird an Ear gu Ierusalem. Bha sinn ag eisdeachd ri fuaim nan tonn a' briseadh air an traigh. Chi mi gum bheil clachan mora gu pailt am measg a' ghuail. Tha mi cinnteach gur e an snaigear beag sin a bha ag ol a' bhainne orm. An do chuir an lighiche na paisdean tinne do'n taigh-eiridinn? Chuir e air falbh iad air bho'n de. Thachair na sealgairean air lorg an fheidh ri taobh an uillt. Thachair cailleach nan cearc orm agus mise 'nam shuidhe air bruach an t-srutha. Feumaidh sinn a bhi togail oirnn a nis. Is fhearr a bhi falbh.

Eadar-theangachadh

A man's coat. The man's coat. Men's coats. The men's coats. A high rock. High rocks. The top of the rock. The top of the rocks. A grey horse. Grey horses. The story of the grey horses. The old man's house. The

14

old men's houses. Among the old men. A sweet song. Sweet songs. A book of sweet songs. A chair leg. The leg of the chair. The legs of the low chairs. A psalm. Book of the Psalms. First Book of the Kings. The big ship of the brown sails. The salmon pool. The head of the salmon pool. The (casting) vote of the chairman.

Who was throwing stones? Yon little fellows were. The Wise Men came from The East to Jerusalem. We were listening to the sound of the waves breaking on the shore. I see there are big stones in plenty among the coal. I am certain that it was that little prowler who was drinking the milk on me. Did the doctor send the sick children to the hospital? He sent them away the day before yesterday. The hunters came on the track of the deer at the side of the burn. The henwife met me as I was sitting (and I sitting) on the bank of the stream. We must be going now. It is better to be going.

LESSON 24

In the last lesson we spoke, among other things, of describing words such as Big, Small, Sick, Long, etc. Now these have their "of" forms just like the name-words they describe and you will find both pretty much the same.

Let us take a Class 1 word to start with say BALACH, a boy. This becomes BALAICH (**bal-eeCH**) of a boy and A' BHALAICH, of the boy. The putting in of the "I" made the "of" form. In the same way we would put an "I" into the describing-word if there isn't one there already to get its "of" form and further sharpen the first letter of the word if possible. Thus BALACH MOR, a big boy. BALAICH MHOIR (**vO-ir**) of a big boy. BROG BALAICH MHOIR, a big boy's shoe. BROG A' BHALAICH MHOIR, the big boy's shoe.

Here are a few other examples:

AODACH MIN (**oodaCH meen**) 1. fine cloth. AODAICH MHIN (**ood-eeCH veen**) of fine cloth. CORN AODAICH MHIN, a bale of fine cloth. CORN (**korn**) 1. bale. FEUR UR (**fayr oor**) 1. fresh grass: FAILE AN FHEOIR UIR, The smell of the fresh grass. FAILE (**fala**) 1. smell. FEOIR (**fyo-ir**) of grass: AN FHEOIR (**un yo-ir**) of the grass. RATHAD FADA, a long road. CEANN RATHAID FHADA, end (or the end) of a long road. CEANN AN RATHAID FHADA, The end of the long road. Note that there is no "I" put into words ending in a vowel as for example FADA, long: SONA (**sona**) happy: BEO (**byo**) living, alive, etc. The same thing holds for those ending in CHD as BOCHD, poor, etc.

Here are two personal names:

MAC A' GHILLE BHAIN (**maCHk a yeelya vayn**). Macilvane i.e. Son of the fair-haired lad; also Mac-Bain and Bain.

MAC GILLE BHUIDHE (maCHk geel-ya voo-ee) MacElvee, Macilwee and Gilbey. Son of a yellow-haired lad.

Now we shall take name-words belonging to Class 2 or Feminines as the grammars call them. Let us take BROG, 2. a shoe: NA BROIGE, of the shoe. The "of" form of the describing-word is just the same: put in an "I" and add an "E" but no sharpening. Thus BROG MHOR, a big shoe. LORG BROIGE MOIRE (lor-ug brOee-ga mOee-ra), track or mark of a big shoe. LORG NA BROIGE MOIRE, The track of the big shoe. LORG (lor-ug) 2. track, mark. Again CRAOBH ARD, high tree. MULLACH CRAOIBHE AIRDE (krooev-a erj-a), top of a high tree. MULLACH NA CRAOIBHE AIRDE, The top of the high tree.

Again, remembering what we said about describing-words ending in a vowel we have

MUINNTIR NA DUTHCHA SONA, People of the happy land.

But FADA, long, and TANA, shallow, thin, become FAIDE (faj-a) and TAINE (ten-ya) when used with Class 2 words.

Ex. FEAR NA SROINE FAIDE, The man with (of) the long nose.

BRUACHAN NA H-AIBHNE TAINE, The banks of the shallow river.

We have already seen how the putting in of an "I" sometimes made changes in the sound and spelling of the name-words. For instance BORD, a table became BUIRD, of a table: CLACH, a stone became CLOICHE, of a stone: FEAR, a man became FIR, of a man and so on. The same thing happens often in the case of the "of" forms of describing-words. Here is a small table which may help you to remember these:

O words change to UI. Thus CROM (krOm) bent, to CHRUIM with Class 1 words. CRUIME, Class 2. Thus CEANN A' BHATA CHRUIM, The end of the bent stick. BO NA H-ADHAIRCE CRUIME (bo na haoorCHk-a krooima), The cow with the crooked horn. ADHARC (a-oorCHk) 2. horn. CHRUIM (CHroo-eem).

17

EA words change to EI as DEARG (jarug), red:
DHEIRG (yayrug) of red; or more shortly at times to
"I" as BEAG, small, to BHIG (veek). Words ending
in -EACH shorten to -ICH. For instance DIREACH
(jee-raCH) straight, upright, changes to DHIRICH
(yee-reeCH).

DEIRGE, BIGE, DIRICHE all with Class 2 words.

EU and IA words change to EI. GEUR (gayr)
sharp gives GHEIR (yayir) and LIATH (lyeea) gives
LEITH (lay) SGEUL AN FHIR LEITH, The story of
the grey man. GEIRE, LEITHE with Class 2 words.

IO and IU words change to I. CRION (kree-un)
small, withered, changes to CHRIN (CHreen).
FLIUCH (flyooCH) wet to FHLICH (lich).

CRINE, FLICHE with Class 2 words.

A few words change A to OI as DALL (daool) blind
to DHOILL (GHoyll) Class 1. and DOILLE (doyl-ya)
Class 2.

Faclair

BLIADHNA (bleea-na) 2. year.
UR (oor) new, fresh.
RIDIRE (reej-ira) 1. knight.
CRUINN (krooing) round.
AIR SGATH (ska) for sake of.
BADAN (badan) 1. clump.
AN DEIDH (jay) after, followed by "of" forms.
SGIATH (skeea) 2. shield.
SGEITHE (skay-ha) of a shield.
BARR, 1. top.
CRIOCH (kree-oCH) 2. end.
TURUS (too-rus) 1. journey.
FADA, long, does not take an "I" with Class 1 words
    but FAIDE (faj-a) is the "of" form for Class 2 words.
EISD! (ayshd) listen!
EISDEACHD (aysh-jaCHk) listening.
GUTH (goo) 1. voice, mention.
LEUGH (layv) or (layGH) read.
BARDACHD (bard-aCHk) 2. poetry, poem.
EANRUIG (ayn-reek) Henry, Harry.
FRITHEIL! (free-hil) attend!

FRITHEALADH (free-hal-uGH) attending.
AITHRIS! (er-ish) relate!
AITHRIS, relating.
EACHDRAIDH (eCHk-ree) 2. history.
GAISGEACH (gash-gaCH) 1. hero.
BEUC! (bayCHk) boom! roar!
BEUCAIL (bayCHk-il) booming, roaring.
FEADH (fyuGH) throughout, followed by "of" forms.
DORCH (dor-uCH) dark.
COMHRAG (co-rag) 1. fight, contest.
TEICH! (chayCH) flee!
NAMHAID (nav-ij) 1. enemy.

Gaelic to English

Aig taobh an rathaid mhoir. Oran na caileige oige. La na bliadhna uire. Ubh circe duibhe. Ridirean a' Bhuird Chruinn. Air sgath an duine bhochd. Dachaidh a' bhalaich dhoill. Badan fraoich ghil. Saighdear a' chota ghuirm. An deidh la fhuair, fhlich, thill e dhachaidh. Ridire na Sgeithe Deirge. Barr a' chnuic mhaoil. Crioch turuis fhada. Crann na luinge faide.

Bha sinn ag eisdeachd ri guthan na cloinne bige. An do leugh sibh bardachd Eanruig Dhoill? Cha do leugh, ach an uair a bha mi a' frithealadh na sgoile agus mise 'nam bhalach, bhiodh am maighstir ag aithris eachdraidh a' ghaisgich uaisail sin, Uilleam Uallas. Mharcaich Righ Seumas troimh 'n (an) bhaile air muin eich ghlais. Bha adharc an taigh-sholuis a' beucail feadh na h-oidhche gairbhe, duirche. An deidh comhraig gheir theich an namhaid.

Translation

At the side of the highway. The song of the young girl. New Year's Day. A black hen's egg. The Knights of the Round Table. For the sake of the poor man. The blind boy's home. A clump of white heather. The soldier with (of) the blue coat. After a cold wet day, he returned home. The Knight of the Red Shield. The top of the bare hill. A long journey's end. The mast of the long ship.

We were listening to the voices of the ittle children. Did you read Blind Harry's poem? I didn't, but when

I was attending the school as a boy (and I a boy) the master used to relate the history of that noble hero, William Wallace. King James rode through the town on the back of a grey horse. The horn of the lighthouse was booming throughout the dark, stormy night. After a sharp contest the enemy fled.

LESSON 25

In this lesson we shall finish with the "describing" words. We have seen how to deal with their "of" forms and now we shall see what changes are made when they come after such words as AIR, on: LE or LEIS, with: AIG, at: O or BHO, under, and so on. We shall start with a Class 1 word, BORD, a table and compare the "of" form and the new form.

Thus BORD MOR, A big table and BUIRD MHOIR, of a big table. CUDTHROM BUIRD MHOIR, Weight of a big table and CUDTHROM A' BHUIRD MHOIR, The weight of the big table. CUDTHROM (**koot-hrom**) 1. weight.

Now let us try BORD MOR with AIR, on.

AIR BORD MOR, On a big table. AIR A' BHORD MHOR, On the big table, the describing word, being sharpened if possible. Other examples: LEIS A' GHILLE BHEAG, With the little boy. AIR A' CHNOC ARD, On the high hill. AIG AN LOCH FHADA, At the long loch. So there is little that is really new to learn about Class 1 words followed by their describing word.

Let us now consider a Class 2 word with its describing word, and as before we shall show first the "of" form then the form after AIR, LE, etc. Take for example BROG MHOR, a big shoe.

LORG BROIGE MOIRE, The mark of a big shoe.

LORG NA BROIGE MOIRE, The mark of the big shoe.

We shall now try out the phrase after say LE (or LEIS). LE BROIG MHOIR, With a big shoe. LEIS A' BHROIG MHOIR, With the big shoe. What we have done is merely to knock out the final "e" of

21

the "of" form in both BROIGE and MOIRE, the describing-word MHOIR being sharpened in both cases.

Here are a few more examples of these Class 2 words along with their describing word:
CLACH BHEAG, A little stone. NA CLOICHE BIGE, of the little stone. LE CLOICH BHIG, with a little stone. LEIS A' CHLOICH BHIG, With the little stone. MHARBH DAIBHIDH GOLIATH LE CLOICH BHIG, David killed Goliath with a little stone. DAIBHIDH (**daeev-ee**) 1. David. GOLIATH (**gol-ee-a**) 1. Goliath. MARBH! (**mar-uv**) kill!

CRAOBH ARD, 2. A high tree. MULLACH CRAOIBHE AIRDE, Top of a high tree. MULLACH NA CRAOIBHE AIRDE, The top of the high tree. AIRDE (**er-ja**). AIR CRAOIBH AIRD, On a high tree. AIR A' CHRAOIBH AIRD, On the high tree.

Take now more than one person or thing.
RATHAD FLIUCH, A wet road 1. RATHAIDEAN FLIUCHA, wet roads. BHA IAD A' COISEACHD AIR NA RATHAIDEAN FLIUCHA, They were walking on the wet roads.

SUIL CHRUINN (**sool CHrooing**) 2. A round eye. A' CHAILLEACH-OIDHCHE LE A SUILEAN CRUINNE, The owl with its round eyes. CAILLEACH-OIDHCHE (**kal-yaCH oyCH-a**) 2. owl i.e. Old woman of the night.

CAILEAG BHEAG, A little girl. LEIS NA CAILEAGAN BEAGA, with or by the little girls.

Remember that we add "A" to the describing-word in such cases unless like CRUINN its last vowel is "I" and here "E" is added. If your describing-word has more than one syllable, add nothing at all. Thus CAILEAGAN BOIDHEACH, Bonny girls.

BORD MOR, A big table 1. BUIRD MHORA, big tables. AIR NA BUIRD MHORA, on the big tables.

FEAR CARACH, A cunning man. FIR CHARACH, cunning men. LEIS NA FIR CHARACH, by the cunning men.

See Lesson 23 — Descriptive words, for CH of CHARACH and MH of MHORA.

The following nine words sharpen if possible the

word that follows them. Here they are and they are not hard to get off by heart — DO (**do**) to. FO (**fo**) under. O or BHO (**vo**) from. TROIMH (**troy**) through. ROIMH (**roy**) before. DE (**jay**) off. MU (**moo**) about. MAR, like. GUN (**goon**) without. GU (**goo**) meaning "to" does not sharpen the next word, however.

FO CHREIG MHOIR, under a big rock. ROIMH BHIADH, before food. GUN CHRON, without harm, harmless. BIADH (**be-uGH**) 1. food. CRON (**kron**) 1. fault, harm.

FO'N BHORD, under the table. TROIMH AN FHASACH, through the desert. GUN CHOTA, without a coat. DE'N BHATA, off the stick. These little words DO, ROIMH, etc., you will notice finish up with a vowel sound and so we say DO'N, ROIMH 'N, etc. FO'N BHORD not FO'M BHORD as the "H" changed the sound of the first letter B to V. This holds for words beginning with B, F, M, P when they are sharpened.

DE is used where there is an idea of something being taken away, that is, a part being left.

GHEARR E MIR DE'N BHATA, He cut a piece off the stick. MIR (**meer**) 1. piece. GEARR! (**gyaar**) cut!

CUID DE NA DAOINE A BHA AN LATHAIR, Some of the people that were present. AN LATHAIR (**la-hir**) present. GU LEOIR DE BHAINNE or GU LEOIR BAINNE, plenty (of) milk.

We have already come across a phrase such as THUIRT MI RI MAIRI AN CRODH A CHUR A MACH, I said to (told) Mary to put out the cattle. If, however, I did not wish her to do so I would have said, THUIRT MI RI MAIRI GUN AN CRODH A CHUR A MACH, I told Mary not to put out the cattle. Here GUN means "not".

Faclair

CRIDHE (**kree-a**) 1. heart.
FALBH! (**fal-uv**) go off!
CRUAIDH (**krooa-ee**) hard.
GEALL (**gya-ool**) 1. bet.

LAIR (**la-ir**) 2. mare.
CLEACHDADH (**kleCHk-uGH**) 1. practice, exercise.
CORPORRA (**korpor-a**) bodily, from CORP (**korp**)
1. body.
AIR SON, for, in order to.
DEAS (**jayss**) right; also, ready.
BUILLE (**bool-ya**) 2. blow.
GILLE-DORUIS (**geel-ya dor-ish**) 1. doorkeeper,
commissionaire.
AOTROM (**oo-trom**) light.
BLATH (**bla**) 1. flower.
SPION! (**spee-un**) pluck!
SPIONADH (**spee-un-uGH**) plucking.
A SPIONADH, to pluck.
MIR (**meer**) 1. bit.
TOMAS (**tom-as**) 1. Thomas.
BONN (**bown**) 1. sole, base, coin.
CAS (**kas**) 2. foot.
COISE (**kosh-a**) of a foot.
AM BITHEANTAS (**am beeCH-an-tas**) generally,
usually.
LAIMH RIS (**laaeev reesh**) close to.
BATA (first "a" long) boat 1.

Gaelic to English

Tha an gille gun phiuthar, gun bhrathair. Dh'fhalbh
e gun fhacal a radh. Tha cridhe an fhir sin cho cruaidh
ri cloich. Bha i a' dol do'n sgoil leis a' chloinn bhig.
Chuir e geall air an lair bhain. Tha feum againn air
biadh math, pailteas de uisge fuar agus cleachdadh
corporra air son a bhi fallain. Bhuail am maighstir an
sgoilear air an laimh dheis le slait chaoil. Thug e buille
aotrom air a' chlag bheag agus thainig an gille-doruis.
Dh' iarr mi air na caileagan beaga gun na blathan
maiseach a spionadh. Thoir mir de'n bhonnach mhilis
sin do Thomas. Bha an gille beag salach o bhonn a
choise gu mullach a chinn. Tha Iain agus a pheath-
raichean beaga am bitheantas 'nan suidhe laimh ris an
dorus anns an eaglais.

Translation

The boy has neither (is without) sister nor brother. He went off without saying a word. That man's heart is as hard as a stone. She was going to the school with the little children. He put a bet on the white mare. We need good food, plenty of cold water and bodily exercise in order to be healthy. The master struck the scholar on the right hand with a slender rod. He gave a tap on the small bell and the commissionaire came. I requested the little girls not to pluck the beautiful flowers. Give Thomas a bit of that sweet cake. The little boy was dirty from the sole of his foot to the top of his head. Iain and his little sisters are usually sitting beside the door in the church.

MAP READING

A very interesting and easy way to remember the changes that take place both in the name-word and the describing-word is to study the Gaelic place-names on the map. Argyllshire and Perthshire are especially good for this purpose and a half-inch to the mile Bartholomew map will give you all the scope you want. You will also see how keen the Gaelic mind is to note form and colour and how exact in description. Let us now stravaig around a bit.

CNOC BREAC means speckled hill. BREAC (**breCHk**) speckled. It also means Trout in Class 1. Thus LOCH A' CHNUIC BHRIC (**ChrooeeCHk vreeCHk**), The loch of the speckled hill. Next take BEINN, mountain, Class 2. The describing-word will go into Class 2 with it. So we have LOCH NA BEINNE BRICE (**bayn-ya breeCHka**) meaning The loch of the speckled mountain. You will note that the first of the two English "the's" is not translated into Gaelic, in this case the one before Loch.

Here is a long one: ALLT GLEANN CREAG A' CHAIT. It means The mountain stream of the glen of the rock of the (wild) cat. You will note that there are three "of's" in the English, but in the Gaelic only the last word "CAT" takes the "of" form.

Now as another example we shall take CARN NAN COILEACH meaning The cairn of the heath-cocks. COILEACH, a cock, has COILICH as its "of" form for one bird, but the "of" form for more than one remains COILEACH. Again FUARAN (**fooaran**), Class 1, means a spring but BEINN FHUARAN. Mountain of Springs. BEINN NAM FUARAN would be The mountain of the springs.

26

Sometimes the describing-word is put before the name-word for emphasis as, for instance, DUBH BHEINN which would mean Black, forbidding mountain. In such cases the name-word is sharpened if possible.

In this paragraph we shall take place-names of which the last name-word belongs to Class 1:

BEINN A' BHUIRD, The mountain of the table or Table mountain. SRON A' CHLEIRICH, The clerk's nose. EILEAN A' CHUIRN, The island of the cairn. EILEAN (ay-lan) 1. Island. MAOL BUN AN UILLT, The bare, round hill at the mouth of the mountain stream. MAOL (mool) 1. Bare, round hill. BUN (boon) 1. bottom, mouth. RUDHA A' MHULLAICH BHAIN, The point of (or with) the white summit. COIRE AN UISGE DHEIRG, The corrie of the red water. COIRE, 1. kettle ; also cauldron-shaped hollow in hill. DHEIRG (yay-rug) from DEARG, red. DRUIM AN UISGE FHUAIR, The ridge of the cold water. GLAC AN T-SAIGHDEIR, The defile of the soldier. GLAC (glaCHk) 2. narrow valley. ALLT A' CHOIRE BHUIDHE, Mountain stream of the yellow corrie. RUDHA (roò-a) 1. point of land, promontory. RUDHA PORT AN T-SEILICH, The point of the port of the willow tree. SEILEACH (shay-laCH) 1. willow tree. CNOC A' GHAMHNA CHAIM, The hill of the one-eyed calf. GAMHAINN (gav-ing) 1. year-old calf. GAMHNA (gaoo-na). CAM, one-eyed; also bent. CHAIM (Cha-eem). SGEIR MHOR A' BHREIN-PHUIRT (skayr vOr a vrayn fooirt), The big skerry of the foul-smelling harbour. BREUN (brayn) filthy, stinking. STOB A' BHRUTHAICH LEITH, The stumpy hill of the blue-grey brae. BRUTHACH (broo-aCH) 1. Brae. LIATH (lyeea) blue-grey. LEITH (lay). STOB, 1. stump.

Now we shall take place-names of which the last name-word belongs to Class 2:

PORT FROIGE, Harbour of (the) dark crevice. FROG, 2. dark crevice. TORR NA CARRAIGE, The round hill of the cliff. TORR, 1. round hill,

27

mound, heap. CARRAIG (**kar-ayk**) 2. cliff, rock.
PORT NA LUINGE, The port of the ship. PORT,
Class 1, may be either a harbour or a small inlet.
EILEAN NA MUICE DUIBHE, The island of the
black pig. RUDHA NA H-AIRDE MOIRE, The
point of the big headland. AIRDE (**arj-a**) 2. head-
land, height. DUN DA GHAOITHE, Hillock of (the)'
two winds. DUN (**doon**) 1. hillock, fort. CARN NA
CAILLICHE, The cairn of the old wife. RUDHA
NA MEISE BAINE, The point of the white basin.
MIAS (**me-as**) 2. basin, plate, or land thus shaped.
LOCH NA SULA BIGE, The loch of the little eye.
BRAIGH NA GLAICE MOIRE, The upland with the
great defile. BRAIGH (**braee**) 1. upland, top of thing
or place. MEALL NA SROINE, Nose-shaped hill.
MEALL (**mya-ool**) 1. hill, lump, cluster. CAOLAS
PORT NA LICE, The strait of the harbour of the
flat rocky ledge. LEAC (**lyaCHk**) 2. flat ledge.

Here are a few more place-names:

BEINN CHARN, Ben of cairns. MEALL
BHALACH, Boys' hill. STOB GHABHAR, Stumpy
hill of goats. GABHAR (**go-ar**) 2. goat.

MAOL NAN EUN, The bare hill of the birds.
CARRAIG NAM FEAR, The rock of the men.
PAIRC NAN EACH, The park of the horses. LOCH
NAM BAN, The loch of the women (note: not
BEAN). CRUACH NAN CON, The stack-shaped hill
of the dogs. CRUACH (**krooaCH**) 2. stack. CON,
of dogs from CU, dog.

LESSON 26

When in Gaelic we say a person "has" a thing we
say it is "at" him. If, however, we want to make it
clear that the person owns or possesses something we
say that it is "with" him. Thus THA TAIGH AIG
IAIN, John has a house, which may be his own or he
may have rented. But THA AN TAIGH SEO LE
IAIN, John owns this house. CO LEIS AN SGOTH
SIN? Whose is that yacht? IS LE DUINE
BEARTACH I, It belongs to a rich man. SGOTH
(sko) 2. CO LEIS? (kO laysh) who with, whose.

LE has many other meanings which we shall see
presently, but we shall observe that it joins up with
MI, TU, etc., just as AIG did. So we have LEAM
(lya-oom) with me: LEAT (lyat) with thee. LEINN
(layng) with us: LEIBH (layv) with you: LEIS
(laysh) with him or it: LEATHA (leh-ha) with her
or it. LEO (lyo) with them. There is a strong form
made by -SA etc. as in the case of RI. LEAM-SA:
LEAT-SA: LEINNE (layn-ya) LEIBH-SE (layv-sha)
LEIS-SAN: LEATHA-SA: LEO-SAN.

Here are some examples of the use of LE in its
various forms:
AM FALBH THU LEAM-SA? Will you go with
   me?
BHA AN CU LEATHA, The dog was with her.
DH'FHALBH A' CHRAOBH LEIS AN T-SRUTH,
   The tree went away down the stream.
CHAIDH AN DUINE BOCHD LEIS A' BHEARR-
   ADH, The poor man fell over the cliff, i.e. went
   with the cliff.
BEARRADH (byar-ugh) 1. cliff, precipice.

LE can have also the idea of opinion or considering

connected with it. IS DAOR LEAM SIN, I consider that dear. DAOR (**door**) dear. BU NEONACH LEO GUN D' FHUAIR AN DUINE AS CHO FURASDA, they thought it strange that the man got off so easily. FURASDA (**fooras-da**) easy. NEONACH (**nyon-aCH**) strange. IS BOCHD LEAM NACH ROBH THU ANN, I am sorry that you were not there. LEIS GUM BHEIL E CHO TINN, CHA BHI E A' TIGHINN AN NOCHD, As (with that) he is so unwell, he will not be coming to-night.

SLAN LEAT AN DRASDA, Good-bye (safe with you) for the present.

MAR SIN LEAT-SA, Good-bye (same with you). Use LEIBH for seniors.

Here are two queer phrases: AN DUINE IS LEIS AN TAIGH, The man who owns the house. This could also have been put as AN DUINE LEIS AM BHEIL AN TAIGH. In the past time it woud be AN DUINE LEIS AM BU LEIS AN TAIGH, The man who owned the house or AN DUINE LEIS AN ROBH AN TAIGH.

One point we have not touched on up till now is, How do we address persons in Gaelic? For instance, Where are you going, Mary? is turned to Gaelic by C'AIT' AM BHEIL THU A' DOL, A MHAIRI? Had it been Jean or Sarah we would have said A SHINE (**a heena**) from SINE (**sheena**), Jean: A MHOR (**a vOr**) from MOR (**mOr**), Sarah. This is something like the phrase O King! which we have in English. In Gaelic the A takes the place of the O of English and the first letter of the word is, if possible, sharpened. Where the word begins with a vowel or F followed by a vowel we drop the A in speaking and usually in writing. Thus THIG AN SEO, 'EILIDH, Come here, Helen. THIG! (**heek**) Come! CUIST FHIONNA-GHAL! Wheesht Flora! FIONNAGHAL (**fyunna-GHal**), Flora. FHIONNAGHAL (**yunna-GHal**).

Perhaps you have noticed that the words we used above have all belonged to Class 2. Those of Class 1 are treated the same way except that we use their "of" form. Take SEUMAS, for example. In addressing him we say A SHEUMAIS (**a hay-mish**). For example, CO BHUAIL AN CU, A SHEUMAIS? Who struck the dog, James? So also we would have A THEAR-LAICH (**a her-leeCH**) from TEARLACH (**cher-laCH**) Charles: 'UILLEIM (**ool-yim**) from UILLEAM (**ool-yam**) William: 'ALASDAIR from ALASDAIR, Alexander.

In addressing more than one person take the word for one person and add AN (or EAN) if this happens to be the same as the form that shows more than one person ordinarily, otherwise add only A. Here are a few examples to make this clear:

CAILEAG, Girl (Class 2): CAILEAGAN, Girls: A CHAILEAGAN!

CARAID, Friend (Class 1): CAIRDEAN, Friends: A CHAIRDEAN!

SEOLADAIR, Sailor (Class 1): SEOLADAIREAN, Sailors: A SHEOLADAIREAN!

BALACH, Boy (Class 1): BALAICH, Boys; but A BHALACHA! not A BHALACHAN.

So also we have

SAOR, Joiner (Class 1): SAOIR, Joiners: A SHAORA!

FEAR, Man (Class 1): FIR, Men: A FHEARA or 'FHEARA!

We can also address creatures and objects, usually in poetry, however, and we follow the same rules.

TONN (**town**) Wave (Class 1): TUINN (**tooing**) Waves: A THONNA.

CRAOBH, Tree (Class 2): CRAOBHAN, Trees: A CHRAOBHAN.

Faclair

CIR (**keer**) 2. comb.
SGATHAN-LAIMHE (**ska-han laeev-a**) 1. hand-mirror.
DITHIS (**jee-ish**) pair.
AN COMHNUIDH (**ung gO-nee**) always.
DAONNAN (**doon-an**) always.
LE CHEILE (**lay CHay-la**) together.
COIMHEAD! (**Koyad**) see! look! visit!

THA EAGAL ORM, I am afraid.
LEIG LEIS (**lyayk laysh**) allow.
CALUM, Malcolm, Calum.
IS CUIMHNE LEAM (**kooin-ya**) I remember.
BAILE-BHOID (**voj**) Rothesay.
CHO MATH AGUS, how well that.
CORD! (**kord**) agree with! please!
NAIDHEACHD (**naee-aCHk**) 2. news (also spelt
   NAIGHEACHD).
AN AIRD AN EAR (**arj an yer**) East.
BU MHIANN LEAM, I would desire.
MIANN (**me-unn**) 1. desire.
IS FADA LEAM, 'Tis long with me, I weary.
TUARASDAL (**toor-as-dal**) 1. pay.
BITHEANTA (**be-han-ta**) usual, often.
RUNAIR (**roon-ir**) 1. secretary.
FANTALACH, dilatory.
TOG DO CHASAN LEAT! Clear out! lit. Lift your
   feet with you.
CHO MATH AGUS, As well as, when a phrase
   follows, otherwise use RI instead of AGUS.
CACH (**kaCH**) everyone else.
CAR MU CHAR, tumbling over.
BRUTHACH (**broo-aCH**) 1. hillside.
LEAMLEAT, with me, with you, agreeing with every-
   body, variable.

Gaelic to English

Co leis a' chir seo agus an sgathan-laimhe? Is
leam-sa iad. Bha an dithis an comhnuidh le cheile.
Thug iad an cu leo an uair a thainig iad a choimhead
oirnn. Thoir an leabhar air ais do'n bhalach leis an
leis e. Tha eagal orm gum bi frasan troma ann an
diugh. Leig leis an duine bhochd falbh, a Chaluim.
An cuimhne leibh an la a chaidh sinn gu Baile-Bhoid?
Is cuimhne gu math, agus cho math agus a chord an
t-aite ruinn. Chan 'eil an naidheachd a tha a' tighinn
as An Aird an Ear cho math agus a bu mhiann leinn.
B' fhada leis daonnan gus an tigeadh la an tuarasdail.
Cha bhitheanta leis an runair a bhi cho fantalach.
Thog e a chasan leis cho math ri cach. Leis cho fuar

a's (or 's or agus) a bha an la, cha do dh' fhag sinn
an taigh. Chaidh e car mu char leis a' bhruthach.
Is duine leam-leat am fear sin.

Translation

Whose are this comb and hand-mirror? They are
mine. The pair were always together. They brought
the dog with them when they came to visit us. Give
the book back to the boy to whom it belongs. I am
afraid that there will be heavy showers to-day. Let the
poor man go off, Calum. Do you remember the day
we went to Rothesay? I do well, and how well the
place pleased us. The news that comes from the East
is not as good as we would desire. He was always
wearying till pay-day would come. It isn't usual for
the secretary to be so dilatory. He cleared out as well
as the rest. With the day being so cold, we didn't
leave the house. He went rolling down the hill-side.
That man is variable.

LESSON 27

Just as AIR joined up with MI, TU, etc., to form ORM, ORT, etc., we find another common little word DO, to (or for), doing the same thing. Thus we have DOMH (**do**) to me ; DUIT (**dooich**, ch as in church) to thee ; DUINN (**doo-ing**) to us ; DUIBH (**doo-eev**) to you ; DA, to him or to it ; DI (**jee**) to her or to it ; DAIBH (**da-eev**) to them.

In course of time, however, people began to sharpen the first letter D, and so we have also DHOMH (**GHo**), DHUIT (**GHooich**), DHUINN (**GHoo-ing**), DHUIBH (**GHoo-eev**), DHA (**GHa**), DHI (**yee**), DHAIBH (**GHa-eev**).

These second forms are now the more usual, though when the last letter of the preceding word is L or N, the unsharpened forms should preferably be used.

THUG AN DUINE UASAL TASDAN DOMH (or DHOMH), The gentleman gave me a shilling. TASDAN 1. shilling.

What we have learned above will help us to form many phrases in Gaelic. To say we "can" do a thing we use URRAINN (**oor-ing**) meaning possible or able, along with IS. Thus IS URRAINN DOMH TIGHINN, 'Tis possible for me coming, or Coming is possible for me, i.e., I can come. IS URRAINN DAIBH FUIREACH AN NOCHD, They can stay to-night. FUIRICH! (**fooir-eeCH**) stay! FUIREACH (**fooir-aCH**) staying.

You will remember how after AN, CHA, GUN and MUR we dropped IS, and so we will have AN URRAINN DAIBH TIGHINN AM MAIREACH ? Can they come to-morrow? CHAN URRAINN (with or without DAIBH), they can't. CHAN 'EIL MI

CINNTEACH AN URRAINN DA A' CHLACH SIN A THOGAIL, I am not certain if he can lift that stone. Lit. I am not certain can he that stone to lift. As we noted before, a phrase like To lift that stone, coud be put, The stone to lift.

In past time we use, of course, BU or B', the U being dropped before the vowel beginning the next word.

B'URRAINN DUIBH TUIGSINN NA BHA AM FRANGACH AG RADH, You could have understood (i.e., 'Twas possible for you understanding) what the Frenchman was saying, ACH CHA B' URRAINN DUIBH AN SPAINNTEACH A THUIGSINN, But you could not have understood the Spaniard. Notice that BU (or B') unlike IS never drops out. NAM B' URRAINN DA TIGHINN AN NOCHD, BHIOMAID GLE THOILICHTE. If he could (were able to) come to-night, we should be very pleased.

Often the "DO" forms are left out and so we may have either PAIGHIDH E NA FIACHAN MA'S URRAINN DA or PAIGHIDH E NA FIACHAN MA 'S URRAINN E. He will pay the debts if he can.

The first form with "DO" is perhaps a little stronger than the second form; both, however, are quite common. FIACH (fee-aCH) 1. worth, value. FIACHAN, debt. A phrase of the form, I cannot see you (him, her, them) is turned into Gaelic thus: CHAN URRAINN DOMH UR FAICINN, i.e., Your seeing is not possible to me. So also CHAN URRAINN DOMH A FHAICINN, I cannot see him or it. CHAN URRAINN DA M' (MO) FHAICINN, He cannot see me: lit. My seeing is not possible to him. CHA B' URRAINN DUINN AN TOGAIL (the stones, etc.). We could not lift them. So we now understand that To see me, thee, him, her, etc., is turned into Gaelic as My, thy, his, her, etc., seeing.

There are many phrases of the IS URRAINN DOMH (or DHOMH) form in Gaelic. Here are a few of the more common and examples of their use. Take, for instance, IS AITHNE DHOMH, I know or am acquainted with. AITHNE (en-ya) 2. means knowledge and the phrase means, Knowledge is to me.

IS AITHNE DHOMH AM FEAR SIN, I know that man.

CHA B'AITHNE DHA AN RATHAD, He didn't know the road.

CHA CHREID MI GUR AITHNE DHAIBH AN ABHAINN RO MHATH, I don't think they know the river too well.

The difference between FIOS and AITHNE is that FIOS means Information, while AITHNE means Acquaintance, though both in English are covered by the general term Knowledge. Example:

THA FIOS AGAM CO THOG AN TAIGH MOR SIN, I know who built that big house.

IS AITHNE DHOMH AN DUINE A THOG AN TAIGH MOR SIN, I am acquainted with the man who built that big house.

Another common phrase is IS ABHAIST DHOMH (or DOMH), I am in the habit of or am accustomed to. ABHAIST (**av-isht**) 2. custom, habit. IS ABHAIST DHA TIGHINN MOCH ANNS A' MHADUINN, He is in the habit of ('Tis custom to him) coming early in the morning. MAR A B'ABHAIST (**bav-isht**) as was usual.

IS FHEUDAR DHOMH (**shay-dar GHo**), I must. IS FHEUDAR DHOMH FALBH, I must go. B'FHEUDAR DHAIBH TEICHEADH, They had to flee. TEICH! (**chayCH**) flee! TEICHEADH (**chayCH-uGH**) fleeing, flight. There is a song whose first line is IS FHEUDAR DHOMH A BHI TOGAIL ORM, I must be going away, lit. To be lifting on me. THOG MI ORM, I lifted on me, I went off.

Two other phrases are very common: IS COIR DHOMH, 'Tis right for me. COIR (**ko-ir**) right, just, also Class 2, a right. IS COIR DHUIT SIN A RADH, You are right to say that. BU CHOIR DHA A BHI FAICILLEACH, He ought to be careful. FAICILLEACH (**feCHk-il-laCH**) careful. CHA BU CHOIR DO'N UACHDARAN NA DAOINE BOCHDA A CHUR AIR FALBH, The landlord should not have put away the poor people. UACHDARAN 1. (**ooaCHk-ar-an**) landlord.

IS EIGINN DHOMH, I must, am obliged to.

EIGINN (**ayk-ing**) 2. necessity, compulsion. MA'S
EIGINN DA NA FIACHAN A PHAIGHEADH,
CHA BHI E TOILICHTE IDIR, If he has to pay the
debts, he will not be at all pleased.

Faclair

CLEAS (**klayss**) 1. trick.
AN LATHAIR (**un la-hir**) present.
ANMOCH (**ana-moCH**) late.
BEACHD (**byaCHk**) 1. judgment; also idea, opinion.
GU BUILEACH (**goo boolaCH**) completely.
COIRE (**kura**) 2. blame, fault.
SAM BITH (**sam be**) any; placed after name-word.
PAIPEAR-SGRIOBHAIDH (**skreev-ee**) 1. writing
  paper.
DUBH (**doo**) 1. ink.
OISINN (**oshing**) 2. corner.
TAMH (**tav**) 1. rest, idleness.
'NA THAMH (**na hav**) idle.
CEARN (**kyarn**) 2. quarter, corner.
SABHAL (**sav-al**) 1. barn.
COSNACH (**kos-naCH**) 1. labourer.

Gaelic to English

Is math is aithne dhuinn am fear sin. Sin agaibh
cleas nach aithne dhuibh. Bha mi a' faicinn nach b'
aithne dha moran de na daoine a bha an lathair. Co
iadsan? Chan aithne dhomh (iad). Feumaidh gur e
coigrich a th'annta. Bidh e duilich an tuigsinn co
dhiubh. Ma's coir dhuit-sa iasgach anns an abhainn
seo, is coir dhomhsa cuideachd. Chan 'eil coir aig
a'chloinn a bhi a muigh cho anmoch 's an oidhche air
na sraidean. Cha bu choir dhuit a bhualadh. Bu
choir a radh gun robh an duine bochd as a bheachd
gu buileach an uair a rinn e am mort, agus mar sin
cha bu choir coire sam bith a chur air. Nach robh
paipear-sgriobhaidh agus dubh agaibh? Cha robh.
B' eiginn domh an ceannach anns a' bhuth aig oisinn
na sraide. Tha e 'na thamh mar is abhaist. B' abhaist
a' Ghaidhlig a bhi 'ga bruidhinn anns a h-uile cearn
an Alba. Chan abhaist daibh tighinn cho trath anns

37

a' mhaduinn. B' fheudar do'n chosnach an oidhche
a chur seachad ann an sabhal. Is fheudar do'n
uachdaran an oighreachd a reic. Chan fheudar idir.
Tha e beartach gu leoir. Tha iad ag radh gur eiginn
daibh dol do'n arm.

Translation

'Tis well we know that man. There's a trick that
you don't know. I was noticing that he did not know
many of the persons that were present. Who are they?
I don't know. They must be strangers. It will be
difficult to understand them at any rate. If it's right
for you to fish in this river, it's right for me also. The
children have no right to be out so late at night on
the streets. It would not be right for you to strike
him. It ought to be said that the poor man was
completely out of his mind when he did the murder
and so it was not right to lay any blame at all on him.
Had you no writing-paper and ink? No. I had to
buy them in the shop at the corner of the street. He
is idle as usual. The Gaelic used to be spoken in
every corner in Scotland. It isn't usual for them to
come so early in the morning. The labourer had to
pass the night in a barn. The landlord must sell the
estate. Not at all. He is rich enough. They say that
they are obliged to go to the army.

LESSON 28

One of the many thousands of Gaelic proverbs runs thus: AM FEAR A GHLEIDHEAS A THEANGA GLEIDHIDH E A CHARAID, The man who holds his tongue keeps his friend. Word for word it is, The man who will hold his tongue, he will keep his friend. TEANGA (**cheng-a**) 2. tongue. GHLEIDHEAS (**GHlay-as**) will keep or hold.

This -EAS form is used after A meaning Who, which, or that when referring to something which may happen in the future, near or distant. The English forms "holds" and "keeps" have the same idea behind them. What we have done above was to take the word of command, in this case GLEIDH! hold! then sharpen the first letter if possible and add -EAS. Only -AS is added if the last vowel of the word of command is an A, O or U. Here are some examples:

CUIR! put! gives A CHUIREAS (**a CHooir-as**).
POS! marry! gives A PHOSAS.
SPION! pluck! gives A SPIONAS (**a speeon-as**).
OL! drink! gives A DH'OLAS (**a GHol-as**).

Here is another proverb which contains good advice to fortune-hunters. AM FEAR A PHOSAS AIR SON EARRAIS, THA E A' REIC A SHAORSA, The man who marries (will marry) for wealth, he is selling his freedom. EARRAS (**err-as**) 1. wealth, prosperity. SAORSA (**soor-sa**) 2. freedom. AIR SON (**er son**) on account of, for, followed by "of" form of name-word. Don't, of course, use this new form after NACH. For example, AM FEAR NACH POS AIR SON EARRAIS, The man that (or who) will not marry for wealth.

Other examples:

AN UAIR A CHLUINNEAS TU AN NAIGH-
EACHD, BITHIDH (or BIDH) TU GLE THOIL-
ICHTE, When you will hear the news, you will be
very pleased. Note the use of TU in these phrases.

CIOD A LEANAS? What follows? (i.e., will
follow).

IS ESAN A BHIOS SGITH AN NOCHD. 'Tis he
that will be tired to-night. BHIOS (**vees**) also written
BHITHEAS (**vee-hus**) shall or will be.

CO A DH'OLAS AM BAINNE? Who will drink
the milk? Note that DH' has been put in front of
OLAS as it begins with a vowel.

CIA MAR A THA THU AN DIUGH? CIA MAR
A BHIOS ESAN AM MAIREACH? How are you
to-day? How will he be to-morrow?

C'UIN' A DH'FHALBHAS SIBH? When will you
be going? Note "FH" is silent, therefore DH' is added.

Sometimes there is a present meaning in these forms.
Thus C'UIN' A DH'FHALBHAS SIBH? might mean,
When do you usually go? The idea is that the action
is continuing right on into the future. Again, CO A
DH'OLAS AM BAINNE? Who is it that drinks the
milk and is carrying on doing so? Take this example:
IS ANN GU LAIDIR A BHUAILEAS E AN T-
IARUNN, It is indeed strongly (the way) that he
strikes the iron. The idea behind BHUAILEAS is
method or practice. THA E A' BUALADH AN
IARUINN means simply, He is striking (of) the iron.
IARUNN (**eer-unn**) 1. iron.

NA meaning that, which or what: MA, if: and
GED, although, take the AS (or EAS) form. THA
AGAM NA PHAIDHEAS AN DEISE, I have what
will pay for the suit. PAIDH! (**pa-ee**) or PAIGH!
pay! MA GHABHAS TU MO CHOMHAIRLE,
FANAIDH TU AIG AN TAIGH, If you take my
advice, you will stay at home. COMHAIRLE
(**ko-erl-a**) 2. advice. GED THUITEAS MI, EIRIDH
MI A RITHIST, Though I fall, I shall rise again.

Consider the following phrase, AN UAIR A SHEOL
AM BATA, THILL SINN DHACHAIDH, When the

boat sailed, we returned home. TILL! (cheel) return! This could also be neatly put by using AIR with its old meaning of "after" and followed by DO, to. Thus: AIR DO'N BHATA SEOLADH, THILL SINN DACHAIDH, lit. After to the boat sailing, we returned home. AN DEIDH (jay) after, could also be used instead of AIR.

Examples: AN DEIDH (or AIR) DHA TIGHINN A STEACH DO'N TAIGH, GHABH E BIADH, After he came into the house, he took food. BIADH (be-uGH) 1. food.

AIR DO NA GILLEAN CLACHAN A THILGEIL, THEICH IAD, After the boys threw stones they ran off. Note the change from English order, Stones to throw in place of Throwing stones.

AIR DO'N CHLOINN SGAOILEADH, GHLAIS AM MAIGHSTIR DORUS NA SGOILE, After the children dispersed, the master locked the door of the school. GLAIS! (glash) lock! Notice how CLANN became CLOINN after DO just as BROG becomes BROIG after AIR, DO, LEIS, etc.

Sometimes the DO part of the phrase is put to the end. AIR CLUINNTINN SEO DO NA SAIGH-DEARAN, GHABH IAD EAGAL, When the soldiers heard this they took fright. AIR DO NA SAIGHD-EARAN SEO A CHLUINNTINN, etc., would also be correct.

Faclair

COIRE (kur-a) 2. fault, blame.
SEALL! (shaool) see! try!
CRATH! (kra) shake!
EARBALL (erub-all) 1. tail.
SUIL (sool) 2. eye, expectation.
CNAIMH (krev) 1. bone.
LINNE (leenya) 2. pool.
THOIR! (ho-ir) give!
SORAIDH (sory) 2. compliments, respects, also
    farewell.
DEOCH (joCH) 2. drink.
MA'S E DO THOIL E (masha do hol a, stress mash
    and hol), please, lit. If 'tis your desire it.

41

MA'S E UR TOIL E (**mash-oor-tol a**, stress mash and
  tol) said to a senior, please.
CAIRICH! (**kar-eeCH**) repair!
CARADH (**kar-uGH**) repairing.
SGUIR! (**skooir**) cease!
STREAP! (**strep**) climb!
LOISG! (**loshk**) burn!
CHO LUATH AGUS (**CHo looa**) as soon as.
DUISG! (**dooishk**) waken!

Gaelic to English

An uair a thilleas an samhradh, togaidh sinn oirnn
gu Ile. Is mise a bhios duilich ma dh'fhalbhas e. Ma
thuiteas an leanabh, Anna, is ann ortsa a chuireas mi
a' choire. Seall mar a chrathas an cu a earball an
uair a bhios suil aige ri cnaimh. Ged a ghlacas e
bradan as an linne an drasd agus a rithist cha mheir-
leach e. Thoir mo shoraidh gu do bhrathair. Thoir
dhomh deoch uisge ma's e do thoil e. Air dha na
brogan a charadh, sguir e de a obair air son na
h-oidhche. Is e Seumas beag a dh' innseas na
breugan. Air do na fir a' bheinn a streapadh, shuidh
iad air a' mhullach. Air leagail na craoibhe dhaibh,
loisg iad i. Cho luath agus a dhuisgeas e anns a'
mhaduinn, olaidh e copan te. Tha mo mhathair air
tighinn dhachaidh.

Translation

When summer returns we shall be off to Islay. 'Tis
I that will be sorry if he goes away. If the child falls,
Anna, it is on you that I shall put the blame. See how
the dog wags his tail when he expects a bone. Though
he takes a salmon out the pool now and again he is no
thief. Give my compliments to your brother. Give me
a drink of water if you please. After he repaired the
shoes he left off his work for the night. It's little James
that tells the lies. After the men climbed the ben, they
sat on the summit. When they (had) felled the tree,
they burned it. As soon as he wakes in the morning
he takes a cup of tea. My mother has come home.

LESSON 29

It must be puzzling to a stranger learning English to find that while I lift becomes I lifted in the past time, I see becomes I saw, I go becomes I went, but I put stays I put. English in common with some other languages has large numbers of these oddly changing words, while Gaelic on the other hand has very few and these are easily picked up.

Let us take a common word namely DEAN! (**jayn**) do! or make! For past time we say RINN MI, I did or made, not DHEAN MI as you might expect. Thus RINN AM BARD ORAN, The bard made a song. BARD, 1. poet. AN D' RINN A' CHLANN UPRAID? Did the children make a racket? CHA D' RINN, They did not. D' short for DO with past time.

RINN (**ro-een**, short) did or made. UPRAID (**oop-rij**) 2. racket.

Again we would say NI SINN STAD AN SEO, We'll make a stop (halt) here, not DEANAIDH SINN, etc. After AN, GUN, NACH, CHA, MUR and NAN, however, we follow the usual way, starting from the word of command. Thus, AN DEAN SINN STAD AN SEO! Shall we stop (make a stop) here? The answers would be NI, we shall or CHA DEAN, we shall not. Note that D and T are seldom sharpened after CHA.

Here is a very common use of DEAN in its various forms. Take the phrase AN SEAS SIBH AN SEO? Will you stand here? This could also be put AN DEAN SIBH SEASAMH AN SEO? Will you make standing here? So also FHREAGAIR MI AN LITIR SIN, I answered that letter could be put RINN MI

FREAGAIRT DO'N LITIR SIN, I made answering to that letter. FREAGAIR! (**frek-ir**) answer! FREAGAIRT (**frek-irst**) answering. Likewise FHREAGAIR MI I, I answered it, could be put RINN MI A FREAGAIRT, I made its answering. The common phrase DEAN SUIDHE! is perhaps more polite than simply SUIDH! sit!

The rest is easy. DHEANAINN (**yayn-ing**) I should do, make. DHEANAMAID (**yayn-a-mij**) We should do, make. DHEANADH TU, E, I, SIBH, IAD, You, etc., would do, make. Remember to drop the H after initial D when AN, CHA, GUN (GUM), NACH, MUR, NAN (NAM), come in front. The H, however, is not dropped out after A, that, meaning person or thing, and GED.

DHEANAINN CABHAG ACH THA MI SGITH, I would hurry but I am tired. CHA DEANADH E IOMRADH AIR A' GHNOTHACH AIR EAGAL GUM MAGADH SIBH AIR, He wouldn't make mention of that affair for fear that you would mock him. IOMRADH (**eem-ra**) mentioning ; also Class 1, a mention. AIR EAGAL, for fear.

The Should and Would form of Action-words can be used to express something between a wish and a desire as for instance DEANADH E MAR A THOGRAS E, Let him do as he pleases. TOGAIR! (**tOg-ir**) Desire! i.e. DEANADH not DHEANADH, Do not sharpen the first letter of the word. TOGAMAID A' CHLACH SIN, Let us lift that stone. NA BEANADH IAD RIS NA NITHEAN A THA AIR A' BHORD, Let them not touch the things that are on the table. Note these two: IARRAM COMAIN OIRBH, Let me ask a favour of (on) you. COMAIN (**komin**) 2. favour, obligation. CUIREAM AN CUIMHNE DHUIT, Let me remind you (put in memory to you). GABHAMAID AN RATHAD DHACHAIDH, Let us take the road home.

BEAN! (**ben**) touch! IARRAM (**eer-am**) Let me ask. CUIREAM (**koor-am**) Let me put.

GABH can be used also in phrases which say that a thing can or cannot be done: AN GABH E DEANAMH? Can it be done? lit. Will it take doing?

GABHAIDH, It can: CHA GHABH, It cannot. BHA
SINN LAN CHINNTEACH GUN GABHADH AN
T-INNEAL CARADH, We were quite certain that the
machine could be repaired. CAIRICH! (ka-reeCH)
repair! CARADH (ka-ruGH) repairing. INNEAL
(een-yul) 1. machine.

Faclair

DLEASNAS (dlayss-nas) 1. duty.
CIATACH (keea-taCH) excellent.
RUIG! (rooig) reach!
AITE-FALBH (ach-a fal-uv) terminal, station, place of
departure.
FADA 'NUR (AN UR) COMAIN, far in your obliga-
tion, deeply or greatly indebted to you.
THA MI 'NA CHOMAIN, I am obliged to him.
DAIL (dal) 2. delay.
TAIR (tar) 2. contempt, scorn.
DAD, 1. anything, a jot.
DEANAMH DHETH (jaynuv yay) suppose, reckon, lit,
making of it.
AIR SON, on account (of), for sake (of) followed by
"of" form of name-word.
AIR MO SHON, on my account, etc.
A CHAOCHLADH (a CHooCH-luGH) its opposite,
otherwise.
LUAIDH! (looa-ee) 1. mention.
LUAIDH! mention!
IOMRADH (1) mention.
RUDHADH (roo-uGH) 1. blush or blushing.
CRON (kron) 1. harm, also blame.
SAM BITH or AIR BITH, at all, whatever.
CHO CRUAIDH AGUS (or A'S, 'S), So hard as (or
that).
TRUAS (trooas) 1. pity, compassion.
RI, with.
AIR CHO FEUMACH AGUS (or A'S, 'S), However
needful that.
FEUMACH (faym-aCH) needful.
AIR CHO . . . AGUS, however, no matter how.
FAICILL (feCH-kil) 2. guard, caution.
FAICILL ORT! take care! Be on your guard!

Gaelic to English

Rinn sinn ar dleasnas. An dean seo an gnothach?
Ni, gu ciatach. Cha ruig sibh an t-aite-falbh ann an
am mur dean sibh cabhag. Tha sinn fada 'nur comain
air son na rinn sibh air ar son. Nach dean sibh
fuireach leinn beagan laithean fhathast? Tha mi gle
dhuilich nach gabh sin deanamh. Feumaidh mi
tilleadh do'n bhaile gun dail. Na deanamaid tair ar
an duine a chionn gur coigreach e. Biodh an aimsir
fuar no a chaochladh, tha mi coma. Bu mhath leinn
ur faicinn mu'n deanamaid dad anns a' ghnothach.
Tha mi a' deanamh dheth gum bi a h-uile rud deas
agad air son an turuis? Bithidh gu dearbh. Cha
deanadh iad luaidh air a' bhalach gun rudhadh. Na
biodh eagal ort, Eilidh, cha dean an cu cron sam bith
ort. Tha a chridhe cho cruaidh agus nach gabhadh e
truas ri neach sam bith air cho feumach 's gum
biodh e. Ni an duine ud ur mealladh mur bi sibh air
ur faicill.

Translation

We did our duty. Will this do? (the business). It
will, excellently. You will not reach the terminal in
time unless you make haste. We are greatly obliged
to you for what you have done on our behalf. Will
you not stay with us a few days more? I am very
sorry that is impossible. I must return to the town
without delay. Let us not despise the man because he
is a foreigner. Let the weather be cold or otherwise,
I am indifferent. We should like to see you before we
do anything in the matter. I suppose that you will
have everything ready for the journey? Yes, indeed.
They couldn't mention the boy without blushing. Don't
be afraid, Helen, the dog won't do any harm to you.
His heart is so hard that he wouldn't take pity on
anyone no matter how needy he might be. That man
will cheat you unless you are on your guard.

LESSON 30

One of the commonest words we have is GO and it changes its form in past time when we say I went and I have gone. Now RACH! (raCH) in Gaelic means Go! but in past time we have CHAIDH MI, I went. After AN, CHA, NACH, etc., we put in a DO to show past time. This DO joins up with CHAIDH to form DEACHAIDH (jeCHy) which we shall call its second form. AN DEACHAIDH IAD SUAS AN CNOC AN DIUGH? Did they go up the hill to-day? CHA DEACHAIDH, No. CHAIDH, Yes. Remember that we never put in a DO to show past time after A, meaning who or that: MA, if: GED, although. MA CHAIDH IAD, If they went. DEACHAIDH is sometimes written DEACH.

In Future time we say THEID (hayj) meaning Shall or Will Go, and it has for second form TEID (chayj), used, according to the rule for Second-forms, after AN (AM), CHA, NACH GUN (GUM), MUR and NAN (NAM) meaning "if". THEID SINN DO'N BHANAIS ACH CHA CHREID SINN GUN TEID IAIN MOR, We shall go to the wedding but we don't think Iain Mor will go. MUR TEID, IS ESAN A BHIOS DUILICH, If he doesn't, he's the one that will be sorry.

Note again that where an action-word has two forms, as for instance THA and BHEIL, BHA and ROBH, CHAIDH and DEACHAIDH, etc., then A, meaning who or that: MA, if: GED, although, in every case take the first form after them. This holds throughout Gaelic.

For Should or Would Go we say RACHADH (raCH-uGH) and we have also the two special forms

RACHAINN (raCH-ing) I should go: RACHAMAID (raCHa-mij) We should go. There is no Second Form coming from the word of command which is RACH! Go!

AN UAIR A BHA SINN AIG BAILE, IS IOMADH UAIR A RACHAMAID AIR CHEILIDH, when we were at home, 'tis many a time we would go ceilidhing. CEILIDH (kay-lee) 2. social visit.

In English we often say of a Business that has not prospered that It went to ruin or It was ruined. With regard to the first of these two phrases you would almost think the business itself had taken part in what happened to it. We have the same idea in Gaelic. CHAIDH AM BATA A BHRISEADH AIR NA CREAGAN, The boat went to breaking on the rocks; or, The boat was broken on the rocks. A, by the way, is here a worn down form of DO, to.

Note.—Although BATA, boat, is a Class 1 word, we usually replace it by I instead of E as if it were a Class 2 word. Thus: SHEOL I AN DE, It (she) sailed yesterday; also CHAILL AM BATA A H-ACAIR, The boat lost its (or her) anchor. ACAIR (aCHkir) 2. anchor.

Further examples:

CHAIDH NA MEIRLICH A CHUR AM PRIOSAN, The thieves went to putting or were put in prison.

AN DEACHAIDH DO CHARAID A MHOLADH AIR SON AN OBAIR A RINN E? Was your friend praised (Did your friend go to praising) for the work he did? CHAIDH, Yes, i.e., He went. CHA DEACHAIDH, No, lit. He did not go. MOL! (mol) praise! recommend! MOLADH (mol-uGH) praising, recommending. THEID AM BATA A BHRISEADH AIR NA CREAGAN, The boat will be broken on the rocks. AN TEID AN T-AIRGIOD A PHAIDHEADH AM MAIREACH? Will the money be paid to-morrow? THEID, It will, or yes. CHA TEID, It will not, or no. CHA RACHADH NA DORSAN A FHOSGLADH ROIMH SHEACHD UAIREAN, The doors couldn't be opened before 7 o'clock. SEACHD (sheCHk) seven.

Suppose, however, in referring to the boat we said It was smashed on the rocks, we turn it to Gaelic thus: CHAIDH A BRISEADH AIR NA CREAGAN, Went its breaking on the rocks; and for the MEIRLICH we say CHAIDH AN CUR AM PRIOSAN, Went their putting in prison. Likewise we could say, THEID DO MHOLADH, You will be praised. THEID AR BUALADH, We shall be struck. RACHADH UR MOLADH, You would be praised (your praising would go). CHA RACHADH MO MHEALLADH, I wouldn't be deceived. MEALL! (myaool) deceive! CHA MHOR NACH DEACH (AIDH) A MHARBHADH, He was almost killed. CHA MHOR followed by NACH, almost. MARBH! (maruv) kill!

You remember that English had another way of saying The Business went to ruin, and that was The business was ruined. This second way is also to be found in Gaelic. We shall use the example of the boat. CHAIDH AM BATA A BHRISEADH can be put BHA AN BATA AIR A BRISEADH, The boat was after its breaking (broken). The AIR here stands for an old word IAR meaning "after". So also THEID AM BATA A BHRISEADH could be put BIDH AM BATA AIR A BRISEADH, The boat will be after its breaking (broken). BHIODH SIBH AIR UR MOLADH, You would be praised. CHA BHITHINN AIR MO MHEALLADH, I wouldn't be deceived.

Note the use of GU and RI in the two following phrases: BHA NA PRIOSANAICH GU BHI AIR AM MHARBHADH, The prisoners were about to be killed.

THA NA PRIOSANAICH RI BHI AIR AM MARBHADH, The prisoners are to be killed. In the first phrase the action is on the point of taking place; in the second a decision has been made.

Faclair

SGIOBA (sgeeba) 1. crew.
TEARN! (chyarn) save!

49

TEARNADH (**chyarn-uGH**) saving.
A H-UILE, every.
NA H-UILE, all.
UILE, wholly, altogether.
BATH! (**ba**) drown!
BATHADH (**ba-uGH**) drowning.
CIS (**keesk**) 2. subjection, tax, tribute.
FUADAICH! (**fooad-eeCH**) banish!
FUADACHADH! (**fooad-aCH-uGH**) banishing.
STOIRM (**sturm**) 2. storm.
MORTAIR (**mort-ir**) 1. murderer.
CROCH! (**kroCH**) hang!
CROCHADH (**kroCH-uGH**) hanging.
A NUNN (**a noon**) over, motion away.
A NALL, over, motion towards person.
RIBHINN (**ree-ving**) 2. lovely maiden.
ARSA, said, quoth.
FIAMH-GHAIRE (**feea-GHara**) 2. smile.
BILE (**beela**) 2. lip.
TIR-IODH (**cheer-ee**) Tiree.
CHA MHOR NACH, almost.
NAOIDHEAN (**noo-yan**) 1. baby.
CUIREADH (**koor-uGH**) 1. invitation.
AN LATHAIR (**an la-hir**) present.

Gaelic to English

C'ait' an teid sinn a nis? Theid sinn dhachaidh.
Bha an taigh 'ga thogail. Bha an taigh air a thogail.
Chaidh an long mhor a bhriseadh air na creagan. An
deachaidh an sgioba a thearnadh? Cha deachaidh.
Chaidh am bathadh uile. Bha an long mhor air a
briseadh air na creagan. An robh an sgioba air an
tearnadh? Cha robh. Bha iad uile air am bathadh.
Theid an tir a chur fo chis. Cha rachadh Aonghas
beag do'n sgoil gun a bhrathair Iain a bhi leis. Co
as a thainig sibh, a chairdean? Chaidh ar fuadachadh
as Alba. Bha na craobhan gu bhi air an leagail ach
chuir an stoirm stad air an obair. Chuala sinn gun
robh am mortair ri bhi air a chrochadh. Cha rachamaid
cho fada agus sin a radh, a Dhomhnuill. An teid thu
leam a ribhinn og a nunn gu Tir nam Beanntan?

" Theagamh gun teid agus theagamh nach teid," arsa a' chaileag, agus fiamh-ghaire air a bilean. Thainig iad a nall as Tir-iodh an diugh. Ged theid mi ann, chan fhan mi fada. Cha mhor nach do thuit an naoidhean anns an teine. Tha mi fada am mearachd mur teid do chur air falbh, leis cho leisg agus a tha thu. Tha mi cinnteach gun deach cuireadh a chur do na h-uile. Cha mhor nach robh a h-uile duine an lathair an oidhche ud.

Translation

Where shall we go now? We shall go home. The house was being (in process of) built. The house was built (completed). The big ship was broken on the rocks. Were the crew saved? They were not. They were all drowned. Last four sentences repeated. The country will be subdued. Little Angus wouldn't go to the school unless his brother Iain was with him, lit, without his brother Iain to be with him. Where did you come from, friends? We were banished from Scotland. The trees were about to be felled but the storm put a stop to the work. We heard that the murderer was to be hanged. We wouldn't go so far as to say that, Donald. Will you go with me, young lass, over to the Land of the Bens. Perhaps I will and perhaps I won't, said the girl with a smile on her lips. They came over from Tiree to-day. Though I go there, I shall not stay long. The baby almost fell into the fire. I am very much mistaken if you are not put away since you are so lazy. I am certain that an invitation was sent to all. Almost every person was present that night.

VOCABULARY

Bracketed forms are to be understood as follows : —

Rathad (rathaid, rathaidean), a road (of a road, roads).
Bris (briseadh), break, breaking.
Cobhair (cobhrach) 2. help, of help.

A

Abhaist (abhaist, abhaistean) 2. habit, custom.
Acair (acrach, acraichean) 2. anchor.
Achadh (achaidh, achaidhean) 1. field.
Adag (adaig, adagan) 2. stook of corn: haddock.
Adharc (adhairc, adhaircean) 2. horn.
A h-uile, every, all.
Air bho'n de, the day before yesterday.
Air feadh, throughout, among: takes 'of' form of Name-word after it.
Air sgath, for sake (of).
Airde (airde, airdean) 2. height: headland.
Aite-falbh, terminal.
Aithris (aithris), tell, relate.
Aithris (aithrise, aithrisean) 2. recital, narration.
Allt (uilt, uillt) 1. mountain stream.
Am bitheantas, habitually.
Am fad's, whilst.
Am measg, among, in midst (of).
An aird an ear, the East.
An aird an iar, the West.
A nall, hither: (coming) from the other side.
An comhnaidh, always.
An deidh, after: takes 'of' form of Name-word.
An la roimhe, the other day.
An lathair, present: also surviving.
A nunn, thither: (going) to the other side. It is also found as A null.
Aotrom, light.
Arsa, said, quoth.

B

Badan (badain, badain) 1. clump, tuft.
Baile-Bhoid, Rothesay.
Balg (builg, builg) 1. bag, wallet.
Ban, of women.
Bardachd, 2. poetry.
Barr (barra, barran) 1. top: crop of grain, a height.
Bas (bais, bais) 1. death: 'a' is long here.
Bas (boise, basan) 2. palm of hand.
Bata (bata, bataichean) 1. boat.
Bata (bata, bataichean) (first 'a' of bata is short) 1. stick.
Bath (bathadh) drown.
Beachd (beachda, beachdan) 1. opinion, idea, attention.
Bealach (bealaich, bealaichean) 1. mountain-pass, defile.
Bean (beantainn) touch, meddle with: followed by 'ri' or 'do'.
Bearradh (bearraidh, bearraidhean) 1. precipice.
Beo, alive.
Beuc (beucaich or beucail) roar.
Beul (beoil, beoil) 1. mouth.
Beurla Shasunnach, 2. English language.
Biadh (bidh, biadhan) 1. food.
Bile (bile, bilean) 2. lip, margin.
Bitheanta, usual, often.
Blath (blaith, blathan) 1. flower.
Blath, warm.
Bliadhna (bliadhna, bliadhnachan) 2. year.
Bliadhnail, yearly.
Bonn (buinn, buinn) 1. coin medal, base.
Braigh (braighe or braghad, braigheachan) 1. upland: top of place or thing.

Brathair (brathar, braithrean) 1. brother.

Breac, speckled.

Breun, foul-smelling.

Bruach (bruaich(e), bruachan) 2. bank, edge, brim.

Bruthach (bruthaich, bruthaichean) 1. brae, hill-side.

Buidhe, yellow.

Buille (buille, buillean) 2. blow.

Buth-aodaich (buth-aodaich, buithean-aodaich) 1. clothier's shop.

Bun (buin, buin) 1. bottom, base, mouth of river.

Bunait (bunaite, bunaitean) 1. basis, foundation.

C

Cach, the rest, everyone else.

Cailleach-oidhche, 2. owl.

Cairich (caradh) repair: also place.

Caisbheart (caisbheirt) 1. or 2. footwear.

Caisg (casgadh) check, restrain, staunch.

Calum, Malcolm.

Cam, blind of an eye: crooked.

Caochladh (caochlaidh, caochlaidhean) 1. change, difference.

Caolas (caolais, caolasan) 1. strait or kyles.

Carach, cunning.

Car mu char, turning over and over.

Carn (cuirn, cuirn) 1. heap, cairn.

Carraig (carraige, carraigean) 2. rock: cliff.

Ceannaich (ceannach) buy.

Cearn (cearna, cearnan) 1. corner, quarter.

Ceilidh (ceilidh, ceilidhean) 2. ceilidh, social-visit.

Cha mhor nach, almost.

Chi, see or shall see.

Cho math, so well or as well.

Ciatach, excellent: also Ceutach.

Cir (cire, cirean) 2. comb.

Cis (cise, cisean) 2. tax, tribute, subjection.

Clag (cluig, cluig) 1. bell.

Cleachdadh (cleachdaidh, cleachdaidhean) 1. exercise, habit.

Cleas (cleasa, cleasan) 1. trick, feat.

Cnaimh (cnamha, cnamhan) 1. bone.

Cno (cno, cnothan) 2. nut.

Cnoc (cnuic, cnuic) 1. hill.

Coimhead (coimhead) see, visit, look, show.

Coir, right, just.

Coire (coire, coireannan) 2. fault, blame. The 'oi' is short here.

Coire (coire, coireachan) 1. circular hollow surrounded by hills ; also kettle.

Comain (comaine, comainean) 2. obligation for favour received.

Comhairle (comhairle, comhairlean) 2. advice: also a council.

Comhrag (comhraig, comhragan) 1. or 2. combat, battle.

Con, of dogs: from Cu, dog.

Cord (cordadh) please, agree.

Corn (cuirn, cuirn) 1. bale: also drinking horn.

Corp (cuirp, cuirp) 1. body.

Corporra, bodily.

Corrag (corraig (e), corragan) 2. finger.

Cosnach (cosnaich, cosnaich) labourer.

Cosnadh (cosnaidh) 1. employ ment, work.

Crath (crathadh) shake.

Cridhe (cridhe, cridheachan) 1. heart, courage.

Crioch (criche, criochan) 2. end, limit, boundary.

Crion, withered.

Croch (crochadh) hang.

Crom, bent.

Crom (cromadh) bend.

Cron (croin) 1. fault, blame.

Cruach (cruaiche, cruachan) 2. stack: rounded hill standing apart

Cruaidh, hard, firm.
Cruinn, round.
Cudthrom (cudthruim) 1. weight.
Cuimhne, 2. memory, remembrance.
Cuireadh (cuiridh, cuiridhean) 1. invitation.
Cuist, wheesht! silence!
Cul (cuil, cuiltean) 1. back of anything.

D

Dad, anything.
Daibhidh, David.
Dail (dalach, dalaichean) 2. delay; also credit re goods, etc., e.g., air dail.
Dall, blind.
Daor, dear, costly.
Dearg, crimson.
Deas, right-hand side: south, ready.
Dithis, two persons: sometimes applied to things.
Dleasnas (dleasnais, dleasnasan) 1. duty.
Dorch or **Dorcha,** dark, obscure.
Dorus-beoil, front door.
Dorus-cuil, back door.
Dubh (duibh) 1. ink.
Duisg (dusgadh) waken.

E

Eachdraidh (eachdraidhe, eachdraidhean) 2. history, narrative.
Eadar-theangaich (eadar-theangachadh) translate.
Eanruig, Henry.
Earball (earbaill, earbaill) 1. tail.
Earras (earrais, earrasan) 1. wealth, goods, property.
Eiginn, 2. necessity, distress.
Eiginn, some. Fear-eiginn, some man.
Eilean (eilein, eileanan) 1. island.
Eisdeachd, listening: from Eisd, listen.
Eun (eoin, eoin) 1. bird.

F

Fad, during.
Faicill (faicille) 2. caution. guard.
Faicilleach, careful, circumspect, on guard.
Faile (faile, faileachan) 1. perfume, odour
Falbh! be off!
Fantalach, dilatory.
Faobhar (faobhair, faobharan) 1. edge.
Fear-ciuil (fir-chiuil, fir-chiuil) 1. musician.
Fear-cuirn, outlaw.
Fearr, better.
Feuch (feuchainn) see, try.
Feudar, necessary, must.
Feumach, needy: also a needy person.
Fhad's, whilst.
Fiach (feich, fiachan) 1. worth. value. Fiachan, debts.
Fiadh (feidh, feidh) 1. deer
Fiamh-ghaire, 1. smile.
Fritheil (frithealadh) attend: also serve.
Frog (froige, frogan) 2. cranny. crevice.
Fuadaich (fuadachadh) banish. chase away.
Fuaim (fuaime, fuaimean) 1. or 2. sound, noise.
Fuaran (fuarain, fuarain) 1. spring.
Fuil (fala or fola) 2. blood.
Furasda, easy.

G

Gaidhlig (Gaidhlige) 2. Gaelic language.
Gaisgeach (gaisgich, gaisgich) 1. hero, champion.
Gamhainn (gamhna, gamhna) 1. year-old calf.
Geall (gill, gill) 1. bet, pledge.
Gearr-osain, 1. socks.
Geur, sharp.
Gille-doruis (gille-doruis, gillean-doruis) 1. doorkeeper
Glac (glaice, glacan) 2. defile.
Glac (glacadh) catch.

VOCABULARY

Glais (glasadh) lock.
Glan (glanadh) clean.
Gle, very.
Gleidh (gleidheil) keep, hold.
Glic, wise.
Gobhar (gobhair, gobhair) 2. goat.
Goliath, 1. Goliath.
Gu buileach, completely.
Gun, without.
Guth (gutha, guthan) 1. voice, mention.

I

Iarunn (iaruinn) 1. iron.
Iomradh (iomraidh, iomraidhean) 1. report, mention.
Inneal (innil, innealan) 1. machine.
Innis (innse or innseadh) tell, relate.
Innis (innse, innsean) 2. island.
Ite (ite, itean) 2. feather, fin.

L

Laimh ris, near hand.
Lair (larach or laire, laraichean) 2. mare.
Lann (lainne, lannan) 2. scale.
Leac (lice, leacan) 2. flat stone, flag stone.
Leag (leagail or leagadh) place, lay or knock down.
Leam-leat, variable, siding with everyone.
Le cheile, together.
Leine (leine, leintean) 2. shirt.
Leugh (leughadh) read.
Leum (leim, leuman) 1. leap, bound.
Leum (leum) leap.
Liath, grey (bluish).
Loisg (losgadh) burn.
Lorg (luirge, lorgan) 2. trace, track.
Luaidh (luaidh) mention.
Luaidh, 1. mention.
Luathas (luathais) 1. speed.

M

Machair (machrach, machraichean) 2. low-lying field or plain.

Manach (manaich, manaich) 1. monk.
Maol (maoil, maoil or maolan) 1. bare, round-topped hill: also bare or bald.
Marbh, dead.
Marbh (marbhadh) kill.
Ma's e do thoil e, if you please: also Ma's e ur toil e.
Meall (mill, meallan or mill) 1. hill, lump, cluster.
Miann (mianna, mianntan) 1. or 2. desire.
Mias (meise, miasan) 2. dish, plate, basin.
Min (long 'i') fine, smooth.
Min (mine) 2. meal.
Mir (mire, mirean) 1. bit, part.
Mol (moladh) praise.
Mor, Sarah.
Mortair (mortair, mortairean) 1. murderer.
Muin, 2. back.
Muing (muinge, muingean) 2. mane of horse.
Muinntir (muinntire or muinntreach) 2. people.
Mullach (mullaich, mullaichean) 1. summit, top.

N

Naidheachd, 2. news.
Namhaid (namhad, naimhdean) 1. enemy.
Naoi, nine.
Naoidhean (naoidhein, naoidheanan) 1. babe, infant.
Nead (nid, nid) 1. or 2. nest.
Neart (neirt) 1. strength, energy.
Neonach, strange.

O

Oighreachd (oighreachd, oighreachdan) 2. inheritance, estate.
Oisinn (oisne, oisnean) 2. corner.
Oran (orain, orain) 1. song.
Ordag (ordaig(e), ordagan) 2. thumb: also great toe.

P

Paipear-sgriobhaidh, 1. writing-paper.

Poll (puill, puill) 1. pool.
Port (puirt, puirt) 1. tune : also port or harbour.

R

Ramh (raimh, raimh or ramhan) 1. oar.
Ribhinn (ribhinne, ribhinnean) a beautiful young woman. 2.
Ridire (ridire, ridirean) 1. knight.
Rudha (rudha, rudhachan) 1. point of land, promontory.
Rudhadh (rudhaidh, rudhaidhean) 1. blush, blushing.
Ruig (ruigsinn) reach.
Runair (runair, runairean) 1. secretary.

S

Sabhal (sabhail, saibhlean) 1. barn.
Sagart (sagairt, sagairtean) 1. priest.
Salm (sailm, sailm) 2. psalm.
Sam bith, any.
Saor, cheap, free.
Saorsa, 2. freedom, liberty.
Seachd, seven.
Sealgair (sealgair, sealgairean) 1. hunter.
Seileach (seilich, seilichean) 1. willow.
Sgail (sgaile, sgailean) 2. shade.
Sgathan-laimhe, 1. hand-mirror.
Sgeulachd, 2. story.
Sgiath (sgeithe, sgiathan) 2. shield, wing.
Sgioba (sgioba, sgioban) 1. or 2. ship's crew.
Sgoth (sgotha, sgothan) 2. yacht.
Sgriosail, destructive, ruinous.
Sguir (sgur) cease, terminate.
Slaod (slaodadh) drag.
Snaigear (snaigeir, snaigearan) 1. prowler.
Snamh (snamh) swim, float.
Sona, happy.
Soraidh, 2. compliments, respects : also farewell.
Stob (stuib, stoban) 1. stake, stump of anything broken or cut.

Spion (spionadh) pluck.
Stoirm (stoirme, stoirmean) 2. storm.
Streap (streapadh) climb, clamber.
Suil (sula, suilean) 2. eye, glance, expectation.

T

Taigh-eiridinn, 1. hospital.
Tair (taire, tairean) 2. contempt.
Tamh (taimh) 1. rest, inactivity.
Tana, thin, shallow.
Tasdan (tasdain, tasdain or tasdanan) 1. shilling.
Teanga (teangaidh, teangannan) 2. tongue, speech.
Tearn (tearnadh) save, rescue : also descend. Tearn often spelt Tearuinn.
Teich (teicheadh) flee, escape.
Thairis air, over.
Thoir, give, bring.
Till (tilleadh) come back, return.
Tir-iodh, Tiree.
Tog ort ! be off !
Togair (togairt) wish, desire eagerly.
Tomas (Tomais) Thomas.
Tonn (tuinn, tuinn) 1. wave.
Torr (torra, torran) 1. round-topped hill : mound.
Troid (trod) scold.
Truas (truais) 1. pity.
Trusgan-cadail, 1. pyjamas.
Tuarasdal (tuarasdail, tuarasdalan) 1. wage, salary.
Turus (turuis, turusan) 1. or 2. journey.

U

Uachdaran (uachdarain, uachdarain) 1. laird, ruler.
Uair (uaire or uarach, uairean) 2. hour, weather, occasion.
Uamh (uamha, uamhan) 2. cave : also Uaimh.
Uile, wholly, altogether, all.
Uine, 2. time, space of time.
Ur, new, fresh.
Urrainn, able, capable.

www.ingramcontent.com/pod-product-compliance
Lightning Source LLC
Chambersburg PA
CBHW070028110426
42741CB00034B/2688